"Jim Wiltens is to the parents of tee
many years to the parents of t
wisdom and practicality."

"Excellent!!!"

— Dr. William Bucholz
(father of a teen)

"I was surprised at the number of times I found myself nodding
in agreement with what you were saying ... combines humor,
interesting anecdotes and clear writing. I read it from cover to
cover in one sitting."

— Dr. Don Taylor
San Francisco State University

"Words that comes to mind: upbeat, practical, and creative, the
fuel I need to get back on track as a parent of a teen."

—— Lois Anderson, Director
Fresh Perspectives Parenting Workshops

"... a recipe for creating healthy and happy young human
beings."

—— Paul McHugh

MONEY-BACK GUARANTEE

Practice the seven motivational principles presented in this book
for thirty days. If you feel the response you get from your children
isn't worth more than what you paid for the book, send it with your
sales receipt, within 60 days of purchase, to Deer Crossing Press,
690 Emerald Hill Rd., Redwood City, CA 94061 and we will send
you a refund for the price of the book.

We're that sure — IT WORKS!

"I would definitely recommend this book to parents of teens and I would definitely read it more than once."
— Rod Wong, Teacher
Bellarmine College Preparatory School

"A user-friendly manual filled with practical tips."
— Mary Martin
(mother of a teen)

"I enjoyed sharing your thoughts and ideas with my friends and relatives. It's the kind of book I want *everyone* to pick up and read."
— Sunny Toy
(mother of a teen)

"Offers a tremendous supply of information."
— John Pemberton
(teenager)

"An excellent reference book for all parents of teenagers."
— Susie Poon
(mother of a teen)

"The structured approach and emphasis on respect for the adolescent viewpoint will be helpful for a lot of puzzled parents."
— Dr. Chauncy Irvine
Psychologist

"Delightfully entertaining. Integrates humor with sensible solutions."
— Pam Breen (mother of a "tween")

"Great book. I read it more than once."
— Dr. Randall LaFrom

No More Nagging, Nit-picking, & Nudging

A Guide to Motivating, Inspiring, and Influencing Kids Aged 10-18

Text and Illustrations by

Jim Wiltens

Deer Crossing Press
Redwood City, California

Library of Congress Catalog Card Number: 91-72741 : $9.95 Pbk

Printed in the United States of America

First Printing 1991

10 9 8 7 6 5 4 3

Deer Crossing Press
690 Emerald Hill Rd.
Redwood City, CA 94061

Acknowledgements

Years ago, my parents, brother, sister, and I teamed up to turn a dream into reality. My mother's vision united us. She envisioned a caring environment that would help children reach for their full potential. Many of the challenges our family faced in this venture were overcome by my mom's determination. Her perserverance and support transformed the dream into reality. This reality provided the experiences necessary to write this book.

Ellen McNeil would be a god-send for any writer. Mix enthusiasm, sprinkle in a willingness to listen, spice with an occasional funny face, add insight, and top with a level head, and she also happens to be my wife.

The editor of the *Bay Area Parent News Magazine*, Lynn Berardo, has always been a pleasure to work with. Her support for a column on teenagers provided me with many opportunities to interview teens, parents, teachers, and others involved with adolescent development.

I want to thank those who helped review the book in its various stages: Lois Anderson, Pam Breen, Kathleen Byrne, Dr. William Bucholz, Peter Elsea, Dr. Chauncey Irvine, Alona Jasik, Dr. Randall LaFrom, Andrew Matheson, Mary Martin, Paul McHugh, John Pemberton, Susie Poon, Obie Pressman, Mike Raffaeli, Dr. Don Taylor, Sunny Toy, Diane Wiltens, Roy Wiltens, and Rod Wong.

This book grew out of a training program on effective ways to bring out the best in children. Originally only a few outline pages, over the years it grew into a sizable binder. Each year, the binder underwent extensive revision with the help of staff and older teenagers involved in the program. I want to thank all the teens and instructors for sharing their insights.

Table of Contents

INTRODUCTION

Assembling A Motivational Bicycle

When I conduct workshops for parents, teachers, and coaches, I start by asking, "What would you like to motivate a child to do?" Some replies are:

"I want to motivate him/her to ..."

... start her homework without me having to nag.

... help with chores.

... be more social.

... do better in his sport, without me having to nit-pick.

... develop interests outside school.

... exercise more.

... show more interest in a school subject, such as English, math or science without my constant nudging.

... be more responsible, or enthusiastic, or kinder, or humorous, or ...

This book presents a strategy for motivating kids in all those areas that concern adults: academic, social, athletic, and character development. If you have ever found yourself frustrated because it seems the only way to get kids to do things is to nag, nit-pick, and nudge, this book offers a positive motivational solution. Techniques in this book will show you how to increase your influence as a parent without nagging, how to bring about changes without nit-picking, and how to inspire self-motivated children without constant nudging.

The effectiveness of the motivational strategy you are going to read about is related to a simple fact — no single technique works every time. Having a positive, long-term influence on behavior requires multiple methods. The seven motivational methods presented in this book reinforce each other, much like the spokes in a bicycle wheel. A single spoke won't get you far. It is a framework of spokes that strengthens a wheel, enabling it to bounce out of the occasional pothole and roll along smoothly.

A parent in one of my classes explained that her teenage daughter was doing well in everything. The mother said, "I'm taking the class to find out what I did right."

A recurring question at workshops is, "How do you encourage children to become self-motivated?" The answer is simple: provide an environment that promotes self-motivation. The techniques presented in this book will create such an environment. Practical applications and examples are tailored for working with children aged ten to eighteen.*

No More Nagging, Nit-picking, & Nudging (A Guide To Motivating, Inspiring, and Influencing Kids Aged 10-18) is based on real life experiences in the family, the classroom,

---

* For simplicity, the words "teen" and "child" are used interchangeably throughout the book and include kids aged ten and up.

athletics, and other situations where adults strive to motivate children. To maintain confidentiality, I have changed names and in some cases disguised identifying details. The techniques you will read about have also been field-tested at a unique summer camp, **Deer Crossing Camp Inc.** Since 1983, Deer Crossing has implemented a motivational philosophy designed to promote the best qualities in children. Many of the techniques in this book are standard operating procedure at Deer Crossing.

Occasionally, I encounter parents who are blunt about what they want from a motivational workshop, "I want to get my children to do what I want them to do." Such bluntness draws chuckles from the audience. But many adults are seriously concerned about manipulation. Manipulative motivation is characterized by closing off a child's options, which is to the manipulator's advantage and the child's detriment. An example of manipulation would be discouraging a teen from taking responsibility by coddling, which might be in the form of providing money, intervening regularly on his behalf, or dominating his decisions to the point that the child is left dependent on the parent. Pressuring a child to drop tennis for football because an adult loves football is manipulative. Guilt-tripping a child into working in the family business, when she would rather strike out on her own, is manipulative.

If there is a concern about manipulation, ask, "Am I limiting a child to satisfy MY needs and aspirations, or am I motivating the child in a way that will expand the child's choices?" Positive motivation encourages multiple options that benefit the child. For example, if you believe that physical activity is necessary for health, you wouldn't limit a child to football because it is your favorite game. You would motivate the child to be physically active by presenting a variety of choices such as: dancing, swimming, yoga, tennis, basketball, ultimate frisbee, volleyball, Tai Chi. If you increase a child's choices, and his best interest is your guide, then you are doing your best. What more can you ask?

In the following chapters, seven motivational techniques are presented. Each is likened to a part on a bicycle. Bicycle parts emphasize the interrelated nature of this strategy. One part by itself is limited. Full power depends on assembly of all the parts.

The shipping container a motivational bicycle comes in contains the following parts:

1. **Perspective** mirror
2. **Communication** horn
3. **Self-esteem** frame
4. **Goal** steering system and wheels
5. **Need** pedals
6. **Discipline** brakes
7. **Attitude** gears

Let's start with the perspective mirror.

1

THE PERSPECTIVE MIRROR

Getting Inside A Teen's Head So You Can Be Heard

The first item attached to a motivational bicycle is a perspective mirror. This mirror provides a different view of the world. A wise cyclist regularly shifts her gaze from the road ahead to the images seen in the mirror. The success of the ride often depends on this ability to shift perspectives.

Perspective can make things easier or it can make them harder. Try the following experiment. Set one edge of a mirror on the line in front of the word MOTIVATION shown below. Place a book between yourself and the word so all you see is the mirror image. Now put the point of a pencil on the "M" in MOTIVATION and trace over the letters.

MOTIVATION

Tracing the word from your old perspective is frustrating. A stubborn brain refuses to change the signals it sends to your hand. The eyeballs and the hands are doing their jobs, but the mind acts like there is only a single interpretation for what it sees. When the brain recognizes the mirror's alternate viewpoint, then, and only then, will appropriate messages travel to the hand. Your success in tracing MOTIVATION depends on your ability to switch perspectives.

Motivating children also requires an ability to shift perspectives, in this case from an adult's to a child's viewpoint. Collisions occur when adults forget to glance in their perspective mirror. In one of my workshops, a frustrated father said, "My son hangs out with bums." When asked if he could think of any reason for his son's choice of friends, the father angrily replied, "He must be crazy because there's nothing he could get from those losers." The father was blinded by his viewpoint. As long as he refused to look through his son's eyes, those "bums" would keep providing what his son needed because the teen wasn't getting it anywhere else.

Adults who make an effort to see the world from a teen's viewpoint are rewarded for their effort. The reward is rapport. When rapport exists, it is as if you are seated next to a teen looking out his window on the world. Seeing through the teen's eyes, hearing through his ears, and feeling through his emotions, you discover what is meaningful to him. Successful motivators incorporate these images, words, and feelings into their communication. Because your communication is tailored to a teen's viewpoint, teens feel they understand and can relate to you. The first step in motivating a teenager is to see the world from his viewpoint.

Understanding a teen's perspective comes on two levels: emotional and logical.

A PERSPECTIVE ON ADOLESCENT EMOTIONS

Adolescent emotions have the same labels as adult emotions: love, loneliness, joy, embarrassment. But teen passions are triggered by different circumstances and, from an adult viewpoint, these triggers seem overly sensitive. A teen's first crush, first cause, and first zit may evoke more emotion than a grown-up can relate to. Insensitive adults tend to respond with the compassion of a Tyrannosaurus Rex. This hurts rapport, a necessary ingredient in motivation. To avoid insensitivity, adults need to *translate*.

Translation converts the circumstance a teen is responding to into a parallel adult experience. This parallel adult experience is a hypothetical event an adult can relate to. It puts the adult in the teen's emotional shoes. This enables the adult to appreciate a teenager's emotions, despite the circumstances that prompted them. The following examples show the use of translation:

Fashion Statement

It's Friday night and your teenage daughter is preparing to go to the mall with her friends. Her clothes are a fashion statement. A baggy, black jacket matches tight, black pants that coordinate with a black blouse that matches her charcoal-dyed hair.

That afternoon you were asked to pick up some shoes at the store. Your daughter opens the shoe box ...,
"OH MOTHERRRR, I can't believe you got me *white*

tennis shoes. That's a ticket to Nerd City. I can't wear these. I may as well forget tonight. I hope you know you've just ruined my weekend."

Many adults have little compassion for the daughter in this scene. Adults may trivialize the emotion, "What a foolish thing to get upset about." Some suggest that Mom should take the offensive, "That's what you get for sending someone else to do your errands." These comments, in the heat of the moment, only serve to worsen the situation. To preserve rapport, translate the teen experience into an adult perspective:

You have planned a large party at your house. Your guests will be arriving at any moment. You feel elegant in a white silk dress. Dashing into the living room for a last minute inspection, you collide with your slow-moving husband. He *was* holding a glass of red wine. Your white dress is ruined. A frantic search through the closet yields a 15-year old maid of honor outfit, color — puce. And, oh yes, there's the doorbell with your first guests. What emotion do you feel?

When adults compare the teen's predicament with the hypothetical hostess, the hostess usually gets more sympathy. Yet if we could surgically extract feelings from the teenager and the hostess, we would find that they are of equal weight on an emotional scale. Different events can trigger the same feelings. Appreciating the equality of emotions puts things in perspective. This opens the way for constructive communication. Let's try another one:

Lunchtime Snub

Your son comes home devastated. His clique at school went off to McDonald's for lunch and didn't invite him. He wants to die. He wallows in misery and doubts he will ever have friends again.

From a lofty adult perspective, you might be inclined to tease or belittle such a short-sighted view of the world. But think how he feels. Translate the experience into something an adult can appreciate:

> You are in your cubicle at work. At noon, you stop in at several of your cohorts' cubicles only to find they've gone to lunch — together. You weren't invited. What emotion do you have?

Emotional translation*

A teenager's emotions are often triggered by different criteria than an adult's. Feelings are important to teenagers. Sometimes grown-ups forget just how important these feelings are. Translation helps adults have an empathetic perspective. Empathy does not necessarily imply agreement. Empathy

---

* For silly hats, you could substitute ties: useless, uncomfortable, expensive. Or how about high heels: difficult to walk, dangerous, poor posture.

creates a compassionate environment in which meaningful communication is more likely.

Teens are going to be irrationally emotional at times (judged from an adult perspective). It's part of being a teen (makes sense, from a teen's viewpoint).

Adults will also act irrationally emotional at times (judged from a teen perspective). It's part of being an adult (makes sense, from an adult's viewpoint).

Learning to switch perspectives needn't be limited to adults. Children can be taught to view the world from alternate viewpoints. Activities which encourage children to look at situations from a perspective other than their own include: drama, improvisational comedy, and debate clubs. Drama and improvisational comedy put children into someone else's shoes and ask them to play that role. Debate requires that the child learn to speak both for and against topics, thereby looking at both sides. You also could pick a topic from the news and ask a child to imagine both sides — i.e., dog bites dog catcher. What's the dog catcher's view and what's the dog's? Establishing the ability to switch roles in neutral situations helps later when dealing with emotionally-charged topics.

A PERSPECTIVE ON ADOLESCENT LOGIC

A common misconception is that children have a functional adult reasoning system and the only item missing is information. Supposedly, if you supply teens with the right information, they will see things from an adult viewpoint. Parents who reason from this perspective are motivationally handicapped.

Kids are not miniature versions of adults. Children think differently. Some psychologists believe that rational or logical thinking only becomes possible with the formation of certain connections in the brain. These connections are still being made in the teenage years.

Child psychologist, Jean Piaget, made many interesting observations to support the contention that children pass through stages in their thinking evolution. For instance, if children five years of age are presented with a physical model of a city and given miniature houses, trees, etc., and asked to construct an identical model, they create a hodgepodge unlike the real city. Seven to ten-year old children can construct a duplicate city, but drawing an accurate two-dimensional map of the model is beyond their grasp. The eleven to fifteen-year old planner can draw a two-dimensional map and also has the necessary intellectual development to substitute symbols for the original objects.

While it is conceivable that a fifteen-year old has the brain power to handle adult thought, in reality, a lack of relevant experience and training may hamper an adolescent in reaching this level until later in life, if at all.

The logic map an adult uses to chart life decisions may be illegible to a teenager. Adolescents view the world from a different perspective and use a different logic. Adults who wish to motivate teenagers appreciate the differences, and modify adult reasoning so that teens can better understand them.

Here are four guidelines for reasoning with adolescents:

1. Reason in concrete terms.

2. Substitute experience for talk.

3. Limit *if-then* logic to one or two points.

4. Use follow-up experiences to prevent backsliding.

Reason In Concrete Terms

Children understand concrete examples more readily than abstract. "At bedtime, could you read *Horton Hatches the Egg* to your little sister?" is more meaningful than, "Be kind to your little sister." If you were trying to get a child to "buckle down and concentrate to get better grades," you would make more headway with, "A and B students turn off the radio, television, and stereo, and work two hours on homework every night — that's what you'll have to do to improve grades." "We're leaving at 7:30" is more concrete than "We're in a hurry." When teens are clear on the direction you want them to go, they have an easier time moving in that direction.

Use concrete examples.

When using abstract terms, define them with concrete examples. Words like perseverance, commitment, freedom, discipline, and effort need to be defined. Abstracts have little meaning for a child with limited life experience. In coaching seminars, I give an example of a pep talk that relies on abstracts and conveys little useful information:

> "O.K. team, this is the time to keep the *pressure* on. Let's show the people in the stands what *determination* and a *positive attitude* can do. I want a *110%*."

Contrast the previous pep talk with the following talk that defines abstracts in concrete terms:

"I want three things today. *Pressure* — that means when we have the ball, everyone sprints to the opponent's half of the field. *Determination* — even if you're not going to catch an opponent, you chase him until they score or we get the ball. A *positive attitude* — if the ref makes a lousy call, you smile. Do these three things and you're giving *110%*."

Defining abstract words with concrete examples makes it easier for teens to understand the coach. When the coach is clear, it is more likely the players will do what he wants.

Motivational language is packed with concrete terms because such terms are easier to understand and respond to. But an eloquent motivator does not always rely on concrete words.

Substitute Experience For Talk

The second way of modifying adult reasoning is substituting experience for words. Words are more abstract than any Picasso painting. A puff of air across the vocal cords is supposed to represent all the sights, sounds, and feelings that occur in an experience. Consider the simple word "cat." If you have stroked a warm Persian, watched the stiff, arched backs of two belligerent Toms, or heard the mewing of a kitten or the caterwauling of a feline, you have an intricate understanding of "cat" that a mere label or word cannot convey.

An in-depth understanding of the word "cat" depends on rich experience. The richer a teen's experience, the more images, sounds, and feelings a word evokes. Reasoning with an adolescent using just words is often less effective than providing relevant experience.

A teacher in a seventh-grade art class substituted experience for talk. She had students sketch a table from three different positions: while standing on a ladder, then seated in a chair, and finally lying on the floor. This was her way of explaining perspective.

Rather than use words to explain what she wanted, a soccer coach attached pie plates to certain locations on the goal net. Players kicked the ball at those targets. Attaching pie plates to the best scoring locations gave concrete definition and experience to her beginners.

Parents who use the phrase, "You don't know how lucky you are," may find that a relevant experience has more impact than words. One family I know volunteers to work in a soup kitchen at least once a year. Their children know how lucky they are. These teens can make comparisons without their parents having to talk-talk-talk. Working in a soup kitchen, babysitting at a day care center for homeless children, or participating in community programs are powerful word substitutes.

Deer Crossing Camp's summer program uses experience in place of words to encourage a variety of traits, such as leadership. For example, to explain the idea that a leader gives positive succinct directions, we play a canoeing game called Pirates and Galleons. One canoe volunteers to be pirates. The other boats are galleons. The pirates chase the galleons. Tagging a galleon adds it to the pirate fleet. One rule says that only the rear paddler can give directions, which the front paddler follows. The success of the chase or escape depends on the captain's clear brief directions, a leadership characteristic. Many teens have never had to think about giving directions or about how another person can best be made to understand what they want. This experience, among others, enriches a camper's understanding of "leadership." When trying to make a point, experience is more meaningful than talk and subsequently more motivational. Experiences are more concrete than any words you could use. Substitute experience for words.

Use experience instead of words.

Limit If-Then Logic

The third point is to simplify adult logic. Logic often takes the form of 'If A then B.' No problem with that, most adolescents can juggle two ideas. The problem occurs when there are too many *if-thens*: If A then B, if B then C, if C then D, if D then E. It's like asking a teen to juggle three or four or five balls. For example, convincing a high schooler to read more by pointing out that reading helps get good grades, and good grades are necessary for graduation, and a graduate has more skills, and skills are necessary for career opportunities, and a good job will lead to a better salary, and ..., is just too many steps. If you want to be a motivational powerhouse, limit *if-then* logic to one or two points.

I had a student who wasn't turned on by reading, but was interested in astronauts. I mentioned that *if* he wanted to be an astronaut *then* he should know that astronauts read a lot when they were teens. I gave him a copy of *My Life as an Astronaut* by Alan Bean. He read the book. On his own, he picked out a book on Chuck Yeager, another famous pilot. Persuasive logic sticks to one or two *if-then* connections.

Instead of this ➡ Try this

Limit the steps in your logic.

Be Prepared With Follow-Up Experiences To Prevent Backsliding

The fourth change in adult reasoning is to prepare for backsliding. You think you've convinced a child to adopt a particular behavior. She even parrots back the logic for her behavior. You think your job is done. Then she does something illogical that suggests complete reversal. Maybe she is saving money, only to blow it on a frivolous item (from an adult perspective). Or she mouths good intentions to study every night, but ends up zoning out in front of television. Backsliding is unsettling, but it is also a standard part of the learning process.

Adolescence is a period of time when children are assembling a personality. Not only must they collect the pieces they want for this personality, they must discover a way in which to mesh traits together. For example, if you have convinced a child that it is a virtue to save money, she still has to figure out how that fits with other virtues. Maybe she has also been taught to enjoy life. If enjoyment means a Nintendo game, leather jacket, or $75 jeans, the adolescent may vacillate between saving and immediate gratification. Adding, deleting, and prioritizing personality traits takes time and patience.

Backsliding can be counteracted by realizing that motivation is not a one shot effort. Patient follow-up is necessary in the beginning stages. Periodically supply appropriate experiences to reinforce traits. In the money-saving example, a child might progress from piggy bank to bank, from bank to bond purchase. Multiple experiences related to saving would then reinforce this trait. Plan some form of follow-up to avoid backsliding.

Instead of this ➡ **Try this**

Have a plan to prevent backsliding.

Using concrete examples, defining abstracts, substituting experience for talk, and being prepared with follow-up make reasoning with a teen much easier. Approaching teens from a perspective they can understand enhances an adult's persuasive ability.

Up to this point everything has been about seeing things from the teen's perspective. What about the adult perspective?

THE ADULT PERSPECTIVE

Keeping one eye on the road and the other on your perspective mirror is not always easy. Teens can be exasperating. As a reminder to maintain perspective, frame these words in your perspective mirror:

> My Purpose Is Not To Win, It Is To Outlast.

This idea, borrowed from clinical social worker Bob Ditter, stresses the importance of a long-range outlook when raising children. The first part of the phrase, My Purpose Is Not To Win, means to refrain from confronting children on a competitive basis. Competition suggests a winner and a loser. Adults are favored contenders in teen versus adult contests. Adults usually have the financial, intellectual, emotional, and size advantages over teens.

But if the adult wins, who loses? If teen choices are consistently directed by use of power, put-downs, denial, or refusing to listen, the child loses. How do children feel if they regularly hear:

- Power: "You'll get in here right now if you know what's good for you."

- Put-down: "I can't believe you're that stupid."

- Denial: "The answer is simply no."

- Refusal to listen: "I don't want to hear a word."

Losers display a variety of traits. They may grow up submissive, lacking inner-motivation and self-esteem, possibly cult candidates. Another possibility is that they rebel in a display of independence with disregard for the consequences. Or they may adopt the same win-lose attitude with their children. If adults treat teens as opponents, adults may win in the short run, but further down the line both will lose.

The second half of the phrase focuses on Outlast. This does not imply quiet suffering. Outlast is a reminder to remain rational. When teen behavior is driving you down the evolutionary scale, back to the amoebic stage of reasoning, consider the long-term effects of your behavior. What do you want for your teenager down the line? What is the best way for *you* to behave to accomplish this outcome?

Deer Crossing instructors practice the Outlast philosophy. Jean was explaining how to rig a windsurfer when a camper piped up, "You're doing it wrong. I took a weekend course last year and they had a better way." Jean momentarily lost his perspective. "Why I've sailed all over the world," said Jean, "in winds that ..." A nearby instructor simply said, "Outlast." Jean hesitated, nodded to the other instructor, and turned back to the teen. "Show me what you learned. Then I'll show you my technique. You pick the one you think is best." This display of respect put a smile on the boy's face. It is interesting to note that later in the summer when this teen was asked by new campers for advice on how to rig a board, he showed the technique taught by Jean.

During workshops, when I introduce the phrase — My Purpose Is Not To Win, It Is To Outlast — I ask audience members to roll back a sleeve and write the words on their arms. I call it a "perspective tattoo." Several weeks after one workshop, a parent called to say, "My husband and I attended one of your seminars. Now when we get into a situation where one of us is losing perspective, the other says, 'Remember your tattoo.' Our teenage daughter looks at us in consternation as one of us rolls back a sleeve and contemplates an invisible tattoo. This secret code has more than once helped re-establish perspective on our long-range goals."

The Perspective Tattoo

THE ROYAL COUPLE OF VIEWPOINT

The Royal Couple of Viewpoint were visiting an art gallery. The Queen stopped at one picture. "That portrait would fit in our library." The King chuckled. "No, no. More suited for the servant's quarters." The Queen took umbrage. "It is a noble portrait befitting our collection." The King's humor faded. "It is inappropriate for a monarch's home." Back and forth they went. Their disagreement was the talk of the kingdom.

People came from far and wide to view the canvas. It became the source of heated quarrels, some siding with the Queen and others with the King. To bring peace, a wise chancellor was summoned. He asked to see the picture. First, he looked at it from the left, then the right; he even scrutinized it while standing on his head. Nodding sagely, he turned to the Queen and asked what no one else had asked, "What do you see in this painting that brings you pleasure?" She described a face framed by tropical trees. The King looked at her quizzically. "And your Majesty, what is it you see?" "Why, I see a hula girl with her hands behind her back." The Queen looked equally surprised. Both stared at the picture, and slowly looks of comprehension crossed their faces.

The Queen saw a face outlined by the palm trees. A prominent nose and moustache are apparent. The visage wears glasses, has thick hair and a beard. The King saw a totally different image. He perceived a cranky hula girl. This hula girl has her feet in the grass (the face's beard). She is wearing a hula skirt (the face's moustache). Her hands are behind her back and her cheeks are the face's glasses. One image, two perceptions.

As a reminder of the lesson they learned, the King and Queen had a playing card designed. This card was added to all decks of cards in the land of Viewpoint. That card is on the following page. (Mount a copy of it on your refrigerator as a reminder to look for both viewpoints.) Depending on how you look at the card, it could be the King or Queen of hearts.

•　　•　　•　　•　　•

The King or the Queen of Hearts,
it all depends on your perspective.

PERSPECTIVE SUMMARY

Use translation to gain empathy with a teen's emotional viewpoint:

a. Pick something a teenager does or talks about that defies comprehension.

b. Imagine a parallel adult situation.

c. Take a moment to experience the feelings your hypothetical situation triggers.

When reasoning with teenagers:

a. Reason in concrete terms.

b. Substitute experience for talk.

c. Limit *if-then* logic to one or two points.

d. Use follow-up experiences to prevent backsliding.

Write on your arm: MY PURPOSE IS NOT TO WIN, IT IS TO OUTLAST.

•   •   •   •

Teen perspective on two-way communication.

2

THE COMMUNICATION HORN

Talking And Listening With A Purpose

Beep, beep, beep. There are three horns on a motivational bicycle. Each represents a form of communication. The first horn stands for *reflective listening*. The previous chapter stressed the importance of seeing the world from the child's perspective. Reflective listening prompts children to share their perspective. The second horn represents *I-messages*. An I-message presents information from the adult viewpoint. The third horn symbolizes *open-ended questions*. Open-ended questions awaken a self-motivational trait in teens — thinking in terms of solutions rather than problems. All three communication methods enhance rapport, a vital element in motivation.

REFLECTIVE LISTENING

In the perspective chapter, emphasis was placed on seeing the world from the teen's viewpoint. When adults fail to appreciate the child's perspective, rapport is lost:

"Mom, work is all that matters to you."

"You know that's not true. I love you dearly."

"You're never here."

"I have to travel for work."

"Don't you care about me?"

"Of course I do. That's why I work so hard, so you can have a nice home, don't you appreciate that?"

"Well yeah, sure, but ..."

"Good. I'm glad that's settled."

The previous dialogue represents a parent trying to "win." The teen's feelings have been discounted; the teen is wrong when measured against the adult perspective. The adult may feel satisfied with the outcome, but rapport is nicked and a small chip falls between parent and child.

If the parent's goal had been to outlast, Mom could have used the communication skill known as *reflective listening*. Let's replay the conversation, using reflective listening:

"Mom, work is all that matters to you."

Reflective Listening: "You feel upset because of my job?"

"You're never here."

Reflective Listening: "You feel neglected because I travel for work?"

"My volleyball team played the top team in the league on Saturday."

Reflective Listening: "You feel neglected because I missed the game?"

"It's like I played my best. I just wish you'd been there to see."

"How about if I set next Saturday aside to see you play?"

"We play the Falcons. I know you'll like the game."

The second dialogue shows two benefits of reflective listening. First, rapport increases. The teen is given a sense that his mother values his feelings. The importance of respecting a teen's feelings was stressed in the section on translation (Chapter 1). The mere act of focusing on what a child is saying conveys a level of concern. Reflective listening requires that you pay close attention to what is being said and then respond in a non-judgmental fashion. This gives the impression that you care. Notice I said, "gives the impression." Many parents care, but they don't transmit this feeling in a way the teen can appreciate. Reflective listening makes sure that a caring feeling comes across.

Second, reflective listening presents teens with an opportunity to explain their feelings. This encourages teens to offer you a seat at their viewpoint window. Seeing from the child's perspective provides information that enables adults to reply in a manner the child will understand and appreciate. The result of reflective listening is an increase in rapport and understanding.

A simple formula for reflective listening is to rephrase comments or criticism so they come out as questions that reflect feelings. Responses should be confined to a single sentence. The tone of voice should be positive. A simple format would be: You feel _____ because _____?

"When is Roger going to call? The dance is only two days away."

"*You feel* nervous *because* Roger hasn't called about the dance?"

OR

"I can't do anything right in English class."

"*You feel* upset *because* of something that happened in English class?"

After each reflective question, listen intently. Listening encourages teens to convert inner feelings into words. Attaching words to emotions takes practice. As an adult, it is enticing to jump in and analyze a teen's concerns. This stunts growth. Teens learn to define what is bugging them and explain their feelings on issues only if adults give them a chance. As Rene Descartes said, "*We never understand a thing so well, and make it our own, as when we have discovered it for ourselves.*" Reflective listening provides teens with opportunities to discover what is behind their feelings. As they clarify their feelings, it makes the adult's task of understanding them easier.

Reflective listening

One of my instructors was working with a very moody fourteen-year old girl. Asking the teen if anything was wrong elicited a standard "I don't know" or a silent stare. At first, it seemed that the girl was simply spoiled. The instructor concentrated on using reflective listening when it was appropriate. After several days, a level of rapport developed and reflective listening revealed the source of the girl's mood shifts. The teen had discovered her father was terminally ill. How you deal with a teen who has a dying parent is obviously different from how you deal with a spoiled teen. Reflective listening opens a window on a teen's perspective. An adult with this viewpoint has a better chance of communicating in a manner the child will understand and appreciate.

The format "You feel___because___" is a good way to start, but continual use of this phrase will make teens look at you like you've got a third eye. A variation would be to make "You feel" and "because" invisible in the reply:

"Mark is such a %#@$&*%."

"You're angry about something Mark did?"

Other variations are to listen silently and attentively, or use short words like "really," "hmmm," and "I see" to encourage communication.

I-MESSAGES

To communicate information, especially in heated situations, use *I-messages*. An I-message explains how you feel without attacking the other person. It is appropriate in situations where outlasting will preserve long-range goals of presenting information and maintaining open channels of communication.

If a child says, "Geez Dad, I'll mow the lawn. You don't have to be such a conehead about it," an appropriate I-message response would be, "I feel (angry, frustrated, hurt) when I get called a conehead. It makes me want to return the (anger, frustration, hurt)."

"Mom, all the other guys can have their girlfriends come over and visit in their rooms. Their parents don't make a big deal out of it." Mom's I-message reply: "When I have visitors of the opposite sex over, I entertain in the living room. It's a house rule I feel comfortable with for the entire family."

On encountering a lock on a teenage boy's room, the father's I-message: "When I see padlocked rooms in a house, I feel a lack of trust. If there is a problem with trust, I want to talk about it rather than see locks."

I-message

When dealing with emotional TNT, leave "YOU" out of the statement. In the heat of the moment, *U-messages* are thrown like vindictive horseshoes in the hopes of wringing the other person's neck. Sticking to "I" will get a message across with the least friction.

OPEN-ENDED QUESTIONS

The third communication horn, *open-ended questions*, rouses the development of a self-motivational trait. This trait is learning to think in terms of solutions.

A teen's problem-solving ability is a quantum leap beyond a child's. It is also a quantum stumble. Acquiring the mental balance to steer a path between intuition, logical thought, and emotional concerns is a skill — like riding a bicycle. Adults

When trying to win, U-messages are thrown like vindictive
horseshoes in the hopes of wringing the other person's neck.

tolerate wobbles on a bicycle, but wobbly thinking is another matter. Maybe this is because few of us understand the intricacies of how we learn to think, much less of how to teach it. Providing children with an opportunity to think through problems is one purpose of open-ended questions.

The following statements are candidates for open-ended questions:

- "I can't talk to anyone about it."
- "School's a boring waste of time."
- "I feel so ugly."
- "I can't do anything right."
- "I'll never make the team."

What does "outlast" mean in these situations?

Problem-solving improves with encouragement. When teens use their problem-solving skills, imagine they are on the seat of their first bicycle. They learn to balance, turn corners, and shift gears by practicing. More practice means a better rider. Parents who use open-ended questions give children the opportunity to practice their problem-solving skills:

"I'll never make the team."

"What prevents you from making the team?"

"Everyone else is stronger and faster."

"Can you do anything to make yourself stronger and faster?"

"I guess I could lift weights or practice running, but that's a lot of work."

"Would it be worth it, to make the team?"

Personal appearance is a major concern for many teens. Open-ended questions can direct them toward solutions rather than helpless complaining:

"I feel so ugly."

"What could you do to make yourself feel pretty?"

The following statement is familiar to many parents. This source of frustration can be turned into a learning experience with open-ended questions:

"School is a boring waste of time."

"What would you do to make it more interesting?"

"Maybe go on some field trips."

"Where would you go?"

"We could go to the aquarium or Nancy said they had a lot of fun stuff at the museum. Maybe we could go where Mom works, none of the kids have seen how they make silicon chips."

"When would you go ..."

Open-ended questions direct children to look for the positive things in their lives rather than accepting depression:

"I can't do anything right."

"Anything?"

"Yeah."

"You mean you can't think of one time you've done something right?"

"Well, sometimes."

"Name one."

"The time I ..."

Here is a tough conversation that was handled with open-ended questions:

"I can't talk to anyone about *it*."

"What's *it*?"

"I can't tell you."

"What would happen if you did talk to someone?"

"They'd think I was weird."

"Who specifically is 'they'?"

"Like Janice."

"How do you know Janice would consider *it* weird?"

"I don't know."

"How could you find out?"

"I don't know."

"Why do you think *it* is weird?"

"I heard some girls making a joke about *it*."

"People making jokes about *it* would be people you wouldn't want to tell?"

"Yeah."

"Is there anyone who wouldn't joke about *it*?"

"Yeah. Maybe someone else who had *it*."

"So, if you could find someone else who had *it*, she might not consider it weird?"

"Yeah. Maybe I could talk to someone else who has *it*."

Open-ended question

Open-ended questions prompt adolescents to seek solutions. Empowering teens to answer their own questions and solve their own problems develops an ingredient required for the development of inner-motivation — viewing problems as obstacles rather than dead-ends. But a single solution is not enough.

Resist the urge to end the use of open-ended questions at the first solution. Use open-ended questions to prompt multiple solutions. Roger von Oech, in his book *A Kick in the Seat of the Pants*, refers to this as looking for the "second right answer." In the world of "second right answers," a pencil is more than a writing instrument. It is a coffee stirrer, kindling, a weapon, a straight edge, and a bookmark. A child taught to seek second right answers develops flexibility. A seventh-grader being harassed by eighth-graders came up with the following possible solutions: punch out their lights, have parent talk to principal, transfer to another school, get some friends together to protect each other, confront the bullies and demand to be left alone. The boy chose the last solution and, to his delight, it worked.

Make it a habit to ask for "second right answers." Asking children for additional solutions only when kids fail to discover the one in the adult mind leaves teens feeling manipulated. Rather than problem-solving, teenagers view it as a guessing game, an attempt to reproduce a carbon copy of the adult solution. This contributes to a meager sense of ownership. If a child doesn't feel a sense of ownership for the solution, there is less motivation to carry it out.

Children accustomed to being asked for "second right answers" do not interpret this request as a critical assessment. The viewpoint is not "Oh, Dad didn't like that solution, now he wants another," but rather "That's one solution, what's another possibility?" Even when the child's first solution is great, ask him to search for others. Encourage teens to give themselves choices. This will also reduce adult anxiety. If a teen's first solution stinks, you don't have to express disapproval; simply follow your habit of asking for another solution. The teen doesn't detect a judgmental veto and an adult doesn't feel trapped by the first solution. Hopefully, with multiple options, the teen will make a good decision (judged from the adult perspective).

Parents often complain that open-ended questions aren't working for them. Further probing often discovers that parents are using open-ended questions that are too advanced for the level their child is at. For example, asking a child how to make school more interesting may be too much for a teen with a history of looking at everything as problems. It is like asking a child on a tricycle to ride in a Grand Prix Bicycle Race. In the beginning, attach training wheels to your open-ended questions. Simple questions for the reluctant student might be: "What's your favorite class?" or "who's your favorite teacher?" or "what does that teacher do that you like?" Over time, develop the open-ended questions, but start simple.

Open-ended questions promote a solution-oriented teen, a characteristic of self-motivators. When using open-ended questions, create an expectation that there is always more than one solution. Use questions that are appropriate for the level your child is at.

USING ALL YOUR HORNS
TO GET TEENS MOVING

Positive communication requires practice. Knowing which horn to beep is a skill. Often you will find yourself going back and forth between horns. The following dialogue is an example of combining all three communication skills.

"I'm worthless."

Reflective listening: "Bummed out, huh?"

"Mark asked Debbie to the prom."

Reflective listening: "You're upset because Mark asked Debbie out?"

"I thought Mark really liked me and he'd ask me out."

You stare at your daughter for a moment. You think to yourself, "Here we go again. They ought to put a choke collar on puppy love ..." But then you remember: *My purpose is not to win, it is to outlast.* So you decide to translate the teen's emotion into one you can appreciate. You think:

How would I feel if I discovered that my husband had taken the neighborhood flirt, Ms. Jacobs, out to dinner? Wait, you think, there's no comparison. But then you remember that from the teen's viewpoint and lack of life experience, she may feel as crushed as a betrayed spouse. By appreciating her perspective, you respect her feelings and you are better able to deal with her emotions.

Translating puts you into a compassionate mood, and you are ready to continue the conversation:

Reflective listening: "You feel disappointed because Mark didn't ask you to the prom?"

"Oh, Mom, what am I going to do? I can't go back to school."

Open-ended question: "Why can't you go back to school?"

"Everyone will be talking."

Reflective listening: "So you feel embarrassed because the other kids will talk about Mark not asking you to the prom?"

"Yes."

Open-ended question: "What would make things better?"

"I want to strangle that weasel Mark."

Open-ended question and encouragement to look for a second right answer: "What else could you do?"

"I should ask Tom out."

Open-ended question: "Who's Tom?"

"That's Debbie's old boyfriend. Oh, Mom, thank you. You are so wicked to give me that idea. It will positively drive Mark crazy."

I-message: "Whoa. I don't want to be known as the wicked heartbreaker. I'd rather be viewed as a heartmender."

"Yeah, I guess I'd just be using Tom to get back at Mark. Maybe I should ask Bobby. Sometimes he acts like a geek, but I think he likes me."

Open-ended question and encouragement to look for a second right answer: "O.K. Ask Bobby out, that's one solution. What else could you do?"

This process of communication builds rapport. Children will feel closer to you. Teens will share their viewpoint with you. When you truly understand where a child is coming from, you have a better chance of influencing where she is going. Because you share her viewpoint, you can communicate with images, language, and feelings she appreciates. You will also be helping teens to develop a solution orientation. Your method of communication will encourage children to see a world filled with challenges and solutions, rather than problems to complain about. Children who think in terms of solutions are much easier to motivate than those who think in terms of problems.

BEEP, BEEP, BEEP SUMMARY

Reflective listening opens a window into the teen world. It encourages teens to share their thoughts and feelings. The insight gained enables an adult to respond in a way that maintains rapport and is meaningful to the teen. A simple beginning formula for reflective listening is: *You feel____ because____.*

I-messages deliver the adult viewpoint without sounding judgmental. This aids in maintaining rapport. *U-messages* should be treated like horseshoes; they damage rapport when thrown carelessly.

Open-ended questions promote thinking in terms of solutions, a self-motivational trait. Consistently asking for "second right answers" increases choice and flexibility.

•   •   •   •   •

An I-message?

3

THE SELF-ESTEEM FRAME

Helping Teens Feel Good About Themselves So They Produce Good Results

A bicycle built to travel long distances needs a strong frame. The frame on a motivational bicycle is self-esteem. Children with flimsy self-esteem are harder to motivate than children with solid self-esteem. Motivators know how to build self-esteem.

Self-esteem is an abstract term. To give it concrete definition, take a pencil, give yourself one minute, and draw a picture of self-esteem. Sketch whatever comes to mind in the box below.

Now, let me try a little mental telepathy. Does your drawing contain a figure with a smiling face or outstretched arms? Maybe your art includes sun rays or musical notes? Does your illustration show a figure on a mountain top, holding a trophy, or crossing a finish line? Self-esteem drawings characteristically include universal symbols for happiness, achievement, and self-confidence.

Compare your artwork with that of three teenagers:

Eric drew a person with a big smile on his face. The person was looking at his own skeleton in an X-ray machine. Eric's explanation was that self-esteem is being able to look at your inner self (represented by the skeleton) and wanting to smile at what you see.

Shawn sketched a locomotive speeding up a hill in a cloud of steam. If a train has enough *self-steam* (Shawn's play on the word self-esteem), it can overcome obstacles. If there is not enough *self-steam*, the choo-choo will be stuck at the bottom of the hill.

Anna had a more abstract drawing. An arrow, representing self-esteem, lies flat on the ground when you are first born. Every time someone does something good for you, it forms a small support pushing the arrow up. The more good things, the higher the arrow rises. The hailstones falling from the clouds represent negative experiences. If the supports are strong enough, the hailstones bounce off.

These sketches and their explanations show that adolescents recognize the significance of self-esteem. Awareness alone is insufficient to assure growth of this quality. *Motivators know how to build self-esteem.*

Self-esteem consists of four parts. Each part is as vital as the steel tubing that makes up a bicycle frame. If you forget to weld

Eric's X-ray man

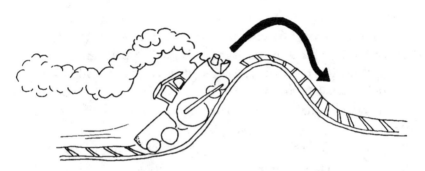

Shawn's self-steam locomotive

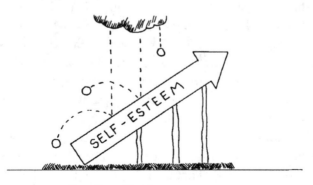

Anna's self-esteem arrow

just one pipe into a bike frame, it will be considerably weakened. A self-esteem frame is as dependent on its four parts for strength.

The four, inter-locking parts of a self-esteem frame are:

1. Positive Belonging
2. Key Words
3. Super Hero's Closet
4. Power

POSITIVE BELONGING

A youngster's first feelings of belonging are centered within the family. Loving parents make children feel wanted. In the tween (10-12) and teen years, these feelings of belonging shift to groups outside the family. This shift is necessary. Adolescents need to establish independence outside the family. Independence enables teens to assemble an identity that is more than a carbon copy of the parent.

There are a variety of groups a teen can belong to (circle the groups your child belongs to):

Family, relatives, community, school, state, nation, ethnic background, friends, scouts, band, community classes (making sushi, yoga, ballet, personal appearance, Tai Chi, jazz dance, SCUBA lessons), martial arts, sports (basketball, baseball, track, boxing, football, swim team, water polo, golf, skiing, volleyball, soccer, field hockey, tennis, gymnastics, ice skating, sailing, underwater hockey), Sierra Club, Audubon Society, 4-H club, auto club, competitive frisbee club, orienteering club, bicycle club, science club, astronomy club, school clubs, religious groups, stamp club, Camp Fire, electronics club, computer club, chess club, guitar club, youth center, honor society, key club, student council, drama club, glee club, choir, political group, ROTC, speech and debate, work (fast food, office help, playground monitor, construction gopher, summer camp staff), volunteer (Red Cross, pet shelter, hospital), and so on. Write in any other groups that your child belongs to:

_____

A *positive* sense of belonging with any of these groups can raise a teen's self-esteem. Notice the emphasis on the word *positive*. Belonging alone is insufficient to raise self-esteem. Let's look at two children who belong to the same group and yet have totally different feelings about that group:

A high school football game is starting. Players are seated on the bench. The coach walks up to his quarterback. "Lance, you've got what it takes. You're the most consistent passer in the conference. I've seen lots of quarterbacks in ten years, but you're the best."

Another player walks up to Lance and gives him a high five. "Lance, we're calling you the cannon. With your passing and my catching, we are awesome." Other players voice similar sentiments. Obviously, Lance is getting a positive sense of belonging.

But there's another member of the team on the far end of the bench. "Hey Robbie," yells the coach, "you wanna' watch the game, go buy a ticket. Let's hustle that Gatorade. I've got thirsty players."

"Hey coach," says one player, "how 'bout we tie Robbie to the goal post after the game?" The coach and the other players laugh.

Robbie belongs but not in a positive sense. Robbie's self-esteem bank account is robbed by belonging to this group.

While belonging is important, it is vital that this sense of belonging be positive. A positive sense of belonging can be generated by using a technique known as *feedback*. Feedback is the first strut in the self-esteem frame. There are two types of feedback. One reinforces behavior. The other changes behavior.

Feedback To Reinforce Behavior

Let's look at two English teachers and the effect they had on a pupil, Tim. Mrs. Fowler was an expert in reinforcing feedback. Mr. Judson was not:

Mr. Judson was meticulous. He was proud of his ability to catch errors on English papers. Tim was less proud. Every time Mr. Judson handed back one of Tim's papers, it looked as if Zorro had attacked the paper. Red slashes covered the page. At the bottom of the paper was the dreaded message: "You need to work on punctuation, spelling, sentence structure ..." Mr. Judson consistently made withdrawals from Tim's English self-esteem bank account, rarely a deposit. Tim considered English a pain. His sense of belonging to this class was negative.

The next year, after a D in Mr. Judson's class, Tim got a new teacher, Mrs. Fowler. She was a remarkable teacher. As the papers for the first assignment were handed back, Tim saw a paper placed on his desk filled with red marks. Here we go again, thought Tim. But this time it was different. The first comment was "Excellent opening sentence. Sets the scene for the rest of the paragraph." The second comment continued, "Good use of the comma in these three sentences." The third comment was "This paragraph created images in my mind." Mrs. Fowler had gone through the paper to catch things that Tim had done correctly. Mrs. Fowler even read one paragraph to the class. She was a wonderful teacher. She had gone where no teacher had gone before. She had entered an English Self-Esteem Vacuum and created the first molecules of English life. Tim went from D's to B's and A's. In looking for what each teen did well, Mrs. Fowler was more than an English teacher. She was a motivator.

The formula is simple. Children who feel good about themselves produce good results. Reinforcing feedback creates good feelings and encourages positive behavior.

The Five Steps In Reinforcing Feedback

1. Catch 'em
2. Immediacy
3. Positive Praise
4. Be Specific
5. I-Message

Catch 'em. Most parents are great at this when a child is very young. You can't wait to catch toddlers taking their first step. Children's first attempts at throwing a ball, saying mama, or feeding themselves are all met with praise. The important point is that you do not expect their first step to be a 100-yard dash, their first throw to zing through the air, their first words to be enunciated properly, or that first spoon-feeding to follow polished rules of etiquette. You concentrate on what they do right, no matter how small. Then you build off success, one small success after another.

Catch teens in the act of doing things right. If the teen is learning something new and getting *parts* of the skill right, give a positive stroke. This is incentive to repeat behavior. In the previous example with the two English teachers, Mrs. Fowler was a successful motivator because she focused on the *parts* that were done well. This focus made students feel capable. Any parent can catch an "A" on a report card, but the true motivator catches all the parts that lead up to that A: studying, note taking, extra credit reports, practice tests, and so on.

Catch all the parts that lead up to positive behavior.

Immediacy. An adult told me how she had been standing in her cap and gown at her college graduation when her father came up to her, threw his arms around her, and said, "I always knew you could do it." Then, she started to cry. She said she wasn't crying out of joy, but because her father had never told her that he believed in her academic ability until she stood there with a diploma. The support came when she no longer needed it.

When a child does something right, give praise immediately.

Sports represent immediate feedback: imagine playing basketball in the fog. You can't see the basket. An electronic basket counter gives you the score after the game. Just how appealing would fog basketball be? Take away immediate feedback and you remove the most important incentive of any sport. Sports depend on the immediate feedback of ball through hoop, pass caught, puck in cage, ball over net, arrow in target.

Positive Praise. Praise should be 100% positive. Check and make sure there are no "BUTS" in your praise — for instance, "Nice job mowing the lawn, BUT you did a lousy job trimming the hedge;" "you've got great taste in clothing, BUT you'd better go on a diet;" "you've got some great insights on this science report, BUT the math is horrible." "But's" leave a stench that lingers long after the praise.

Adults may not be aware they use "buts" in their praise. Mrs. Clemmens had just praised her child. The daughter continued to look at her expectantly. "What is it, dear?" said Mrs. Clemmens. Her daughter replied, "Where's the 'but'?" Her daughter had become so accustomed to "but's" that she automatically expected one. Mrs. Clemmens was careful to leave "buts" out of her praise from then on.

Similar to "but" praise is negative praise. This is the kind of praise where negative comments are added to positive comments. The result is zero. "Sally, you used to be such a slob. Your room really looks neat." "Thanks for not blasting out my eardrums with that stereo." "Who would've thought such an ugly duckling could look so cute?"

Quality praise is positive praise.

Be Specific. *This is the most important part of feedback.* If you want teens to repeat a particular action, tell them specifically what action was good.

Rate the following sentences by circling those statements that represent specific feedback:

a. "You are the most wonderful child a mother could have."

b. "No one does a better job of mowing the lawn than you."

c. "Hanging up clothes in the closet makes the room look organized."

d. "That's initiative — three mornings you've gotten up on your own."

e. "What a hard worker, two hours of homework before dinner."

f. "When you smile like that it makes everyone in the room feel your warmth."

g. "Having you on the team is a real asset. Your behavior is exemplary."

(Statements c, d, e, and f are specific)

If it isn't specific, it isn't reinforcing feedback.

Statements open to multiple interpretations indicate non-specific feedback. A director given a script entitled "You are the most wonderful child a mother could have" gets a script with hazy guidelines. The movie could be child defends mother against heinous landlord, or child gives Mom winning lottery ticket, or child hugs Dad, or child finally picks up dirty gym socks. Statements open to multiple interpretations do not reinforce specific behavior. Being concrete and specific about what a child does well is the best way to guarantee more of that same behavior.

A parent in one of my workshops was having difficulty with feedback. She was convinced it didn't work. "When my son comes down for breakfast in the morning," she said, "I tell him what a wonderful kid he is. Or he will come home after school and I'll tell him he's dynamite. I always get a snotty look in return. He doesn't value praise from me." When asked if her praise applied to anything in particular, Mom admitted that she wasn't focused on anything specific. Lack of specificity robs praise of its motivational value. Making an effort to discover what a teen does well makes praise valuable. This doesn't mean you stop giving your child the 'You're-a-wonderful-kid' kind of compliment. Maybe twenty-five percent of your praise is non-specific; reserve the other seventy-five percent of your praise for specific feedback.

I-Message. In the chapter on communication, I-messages were used to deliver information in a non-judgmental fashion. I-messages used in feedback add sincerity. They are your reasons for feeling that a particular behavior is good.

- "The pink blouse brings out the rose in your cheeks. *I think you look beautiful.*"

- "Baking cookies and cleaning the house before the party took a lot of pressure off me. *I really appreciate the help.*"

- "The garage was swept and the tools put away. *I like that after a job. It means I can get the car in the garage.*"

Reinforcing feedback is specific and followed by an I-message.

Effective reinforcing feedback covers one specific item in two to three sentences. Too many items or too many words and feedback loses its pizzazz. To be memorable, feedback is kept short like a well written poem. The poet concentrates all her sights, sounds and emotions into a few carefully chosen words. Keep compliments short. Think of feedback as the poetry of motivation — less is more.

Reinforcing Feedback Shapes Lives

Reinforcing feedback shapes lives. Consider the following stories from three adults:

"As a child, I always considered myself an ugly duckling. Then one Halloween, all made up for trick-or-treating, I visited a friend's house. My friend's mother came to the door and told me, "Why you applied that lipstick so perfectly, it makes you look like quite a lady." Of course at eight, I knew practically nothing about lipstick, but I had tried to put it on very carefully. I never forgot what she said. It helped to validate that I was pretty and, to my young mind, it established that I was feminine."

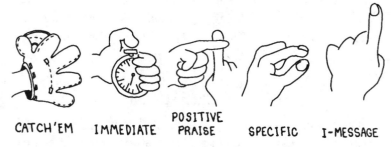

CATCH'EM   IMMEDIATE   POSITIVE PRAISE   SPECIFIC   I-MESSAGE

Reinforcing feedback in the palm of your hand

Praise often has an impact that goes beyond the moment. A father in one of my seminars related this story from his childhood:

> "I took a telephone call from a relative for my mother who wasn't home at the time. Later in the week, that relative called back and told my mother how impressed he had been by the courtesy and politeness I displayed. My mother passed on this gem of praise. It may be one reason I went into management work. At a young age, I saw myself as a person who others appreciated for diplomacy and courtesy."

Another mother relates how a bit of praise helped to shape her personality:

> "I was a shy child. Then, in seventh grade, I got a part in a musical. When I got off the stage, the teacher told me I had stolen the show with the song I had sung. I have never forgotten that."

The mother told this story in front of a group. Her relaxed and enthusiastic attitude didn't show a shadow of the shy child from years ago.

A simple instance of praise from years ago remains etched in these adults' memories. Reinforcing feedback molds more than a smile. It shapes image. Children rise to the heights when given rungs of praise to climb on.

Feedback To Change Behavior

Posture, courtesy, diet, exercise, throwing a baseball, punctuation on essays, reading skills, study habits, personal grooming ... How can you change a teen's behavior in these areas and still maintain a positive sense of belonging?

Mr. Walters pulls into his driveway and sees the lawn mower sitting in the middle of an unmown lawn. He slams the car door. When he enters the house, he sees his daughter sprawled on the couch, watching *Gilligan's Island*. "Marcie, you are the laziest teenager I have ever seen. I work all day and you can't even ..."

Contrast this first scenario with: Mr. Walters pulls into his driveway. Seeing the lawn mower sitting in the middle of an unmown lawn, he starts to slam the car door, then he hesitates. Looking strangely at his arm, he rolls back his sleeve and stares at an invisible tattoo — My Purpose Is Not To Win, It Is To Outlast. A minute later, he walks into the house. "Marcie, I see you took the initiative to get the lawn mower ready. Please mow the lawn before dinner. A cut lawn satisfies my sense of order, but I'm usually too beat to do it when I get home."

What did Mr. Walters want? Both techniques may get the lawn mown. Only one maintains a positive sense of belonging. When Mr. Walters uses feedback instead of hurtful criticism, he will accomplish two goals. He retains rapport, and 90% of the time this is all it takes to get the job done.

Four Steps To Change Behavior

Feedback to change behavior contains four distinct steps. Three of those steps are similar to steps in reinforcing feedback:

1. Be Specific.
2. Tell 'em, Show 'em, Coach 'em.
3. Be Positive.
4. I-Message (optional).

Be Specific. Be specific about what you want. In the previous section on reinforcing feedback, emphasis was placed on giving specific praise. Specific praise encourages a teen to repeat behavior you value. When you want to change behavior, being specific is equally important. If you are talking to a teen and want to have the most motivational impact, explain what you want to have happen in clear concrete terms:

- "Please pick up your gym clothes and put them in the hamper before dinner."

- "Stretch your arm as far back behind your body as it will go, then throw the ball."

- "Put your birthday presents on the hall table. You'll find a stack of thank you notes. Write a thank you note. Then you can take the gift to your room."

As a practical example of changing behavior by being specific, let's go to a swim class:

Todd was teaching more kids to swim than the other instructors. His secret: "Focus teaching time on the correct way to stroke, breathe, or kick. *Don't waste time telling kids what they do wrong.*" If a child makes a mistake, give clear directions about the right way to do it. He then demonstrated his technique with a student:

"Pull your hand back until your thumb touches the bottom of your bathing suit," said Todd. "Watch me. Now you do it. Did your thumb touch your suit?"

If the child repeated a mistake, Todd would switch to an alternate method, always concentrating on the correct way to do the motion.

"Here, let me hold your hand and I'll pull it through the water for you. Can you feel how your arm stretches out before your hand lifts out of the water?"

To Todd, being specific meant focusing all his teaching energy on the *correct* way to do things.

You will notice that Todd used more than words to get across his lesson. Sometimes he found that showing the child or actually doing something physical, like pulling the child's hand through a stroke, was more effective than words. This takes us to the next step in changing behavior.

Tell 'em, Show 'em, Coach 'em. Adults usually think in terms of changing behavior by telling someone how to do something. Yet verbal directions may be the least effective method for motivating behavior change.

To make this point during instructor training at Deer Crossing Camp, we set up the following experience/experiment. Four volunteer students wait outside the room. The instructor's job is to teach the students a skill, for example, a kayak stroke. But the instructor is limited to verbal directions with the first student, visual with the second, kinesthetic (physical) with the third, and a combination of all three methods with the last student. The first student enters the room blindfolded. The instructor must rely on words to teach a kayak stroke. The student makes many mistakes before getting it right. The second student has an easier time. He can watch while the instructor demonstrates. "Show 'em" produces results more quickly than "tell 'em." The last student, also blindfolded, is coached by placing a paddle in her hands that is pulled by the instructor through the desired stroking motion. "Coach 'em" produces results more quickly than the other two methods. The final student gets the benefit of all three methods. The instructor shows 'em, tells 'em, and coaches 'em. The final student learns the fastest.

Tell 'em is good. Tell 'em and show 'em is better. Tell 'em, show 'em, and coach 'em is best. Combining techniques increases the speed at which behavioral change occurs.

Tell 'em, show 'em, and coach 'em.

Be Positive. This is related to the "no-buts" in reinforcing feedback. Being positive can be accomplished by having an upbeat tone in your voice, punctuating your sentence with a smile, or giving a pat on the back. You can also add a positive statement:

- "That's a championship swing with the arms. Now pivot with the hips."

- "When you have buddies over, entertain in your room. *If you get any more popular, we'll have to build you a bigger room.*"

The purpose of being positive is to build a positive sense of belonging. Super-motivators have the ability not only to change behavior but to enhance rapport and build self-esteem in the process.

I-Messages. (See Chapter 2, as well as the previous section on reinforcing feedback.) For changing behavior with feedback, I-messages are optional. When a child values the change you are trying to bring about, an I-message is unnecessary. If a teen wants to play the guitar or pitch a baseball faster or foxtrot for the school prom, there is an openness to change. Any positive feedback you give will be appreciated.

An I-message becomes necessary when the teen is resistant to change. In this case, the I-message states why you value a certain behavior:

- "Before dinner, please go through the kitchen and living room and pick up anything that belongs to you and put it in your room. *I like an orderly house. It's easier for me to clean and keep track of things.*"

- "Please be ready for church at 11:00. The sermon is on having the strength to deal with tough times. *I want my children to have that strength.*"

- "Find a parent to chaperone the trip, and you can go. *I feel an adult won't get in the way of activities I approve of.*"

- "When you're eighteen, you can decide whether or not to buy a car. *I think a car offers too many distractions in high school.*"

An I-message, used in conjunction with changing behavior, clarifies values. If rapport exists, a teen will consider the adult viewpoint. The teen may accept the adult's reason, or the teen may change behavior because she values the relationship and understands the significance the adult attaches to the change.

When A Change Starts, Return To Reinforcing Feedback

When a change in behavior starts to occur, the new behavior should be strengthened with reinforcing feedback: catch 'em immediately and use positive, specific praise plus an I-message. To illustrate, if a child begins to respond to your suggestion to improve his posture by standing like he is balancing a book on his head, catch these examples of good posture and praise them, "I think a straight back makes you look strong." Following a change in behavior with reinforcing feedback completes the change loop.

Inner Coach

Feedback comes in two forms. One reinforces and one changes behavior, but both contribute to a positive sense of belonging. Feedback also boosts self-motivation. Every child has an inner coach. These coaches run the gamut from being very critical to very supportive. Children raised with positive feedback develop an inner coach that concentrates on what they do well. Their personal coach also tells them to improve their behavior through specific actions. These inner-feedback coaches are supportive. Their pep talks sound something like this:

"An hour every day this week on math homework is a real improvement. My quiz grades have gone from C's to B's. Now I have to do something about Spanish. I think I'll learn twenty new words every day between now and the test on Thursday."

Positive feedback from the outside encourages feedback from the inside. When children's self-talk emphasizes their successes and prompts them to think in terms of solutions, teens motivate themselves. Feedback trains a child to have a supportive inner coach.

Feedback is a powerful motivational tool. That may be why experts call it the "breakfast of champions."

Maximizing Belonging:
Avoiding The Corral Syndrome

If positive association with one group is beneficial, even more rewarding is a positive sense of belonging to multiple groups. In the beginning of this section, a list of groups was presented. Unfortunately, a self-limiting trait sprouts in adolescence that inhibits venturing into new groups — self-consciousness. Self-consciousness is the price teens pay for their expanded mental capacity. A teenager can think about what others think about them. As children, they were relatively unconcerned about what others thought. A three-year old can run gleefully through a restaurant, screaming at the top of her lungs, but few teens would be caught dead displaying such behavior. This is because a teen can think about what the patrons would think. In this instance, an awareness of what others think promotes social acceptability. Problems occur when teens are excessively self-conscious. A teen who is ruled by "be cool or be the fool" is ruled by a fear of making social blunders. This fear leads to the *corral syndrome*.

The corral syndrome describes the behavior of a teen who selects a homogeneous group of friends. Friends are cemented into the relationship like posts in a corral. Barbed wire is strung between the posts and the gate is closed. These corrals have signs. They read: Nerds, Jocks, Stoners, Cheerleaders, Preppies, Mods, Rockers, Surfers, Mallies (kids who hang out in malls),

Dweebs (synonym for nerd), Greasers, Normies, Skaters, Brains, etc.

The initial introduction into any new group is preceded by a level of discomfort: "Am I dressed right, what should I say, why is everyone looking at me?" Eventually, the group's etiquette is learned and the comfort level goes up. Overly-sensitive teenagers, once accepted in a group, avoid exposing themselves to that first level of discomfort again. They escape unfamiliar social situations by associating only with members of their clique.

Children, stereotyped in a single corral, limit their self-esteem. Corral syndrome children feed in a single pasture. They are content to munch on the same hay month after month. Thoroughbreds, on the other hand, feed in many fields. Champions need oats, alfalfa, wheat, and the occasional carrot or apple. Remember Lance, the quarterback mentioned earlier? He could rub shoulders with the best of them on the athletic field. How would he do in the drama or electronics club? Would he call them wimps and nerds? Is his self-confidence narrowly limited to the football field? Imagine that Lance could talk with the brains in his computer club, occasionally volunteered at a home for the elderly, and had a part in a community play, *A Midsummer Night's Dream*. How much richer would his sense of belonging be?

Self-esteem grows by venturing into new pastures. The O.K. corral has an open gate.

A teen in one of my classes had a good question, "What if I am happy and satisfied with the clique I'm in? Why should I make other friends?" The answer is simple. Our world changes rapidly. A lack of flexibility restricts a teen's options. It's no coincidence that literature and movies are filled with characters like the one-sided, star athlete in high school who winds up a disillusioned adult. Venturing into new corrals builds social courage, an important ingredient in a society that changes more rapidly every year.

What are some corrals you can stimulate teens to visit?

Attend: plays, nature hikes, community education classes (sushi, ballet, modeling, karate, photography, personal improvement, sign language, guitar, yoga, fencing, cartooning, auto maintenance).

Visit: museums (car, art, anthropological, surfer, American Indian, dinosaur, natural history, Egyptian, local societies, airplane), colleges, planetarium, zoo, aquarium, local festivals.

Vacation: go to summer camp, visit a foreign land and live with another family, spend a vacation on a working farm, go on an archaeological expedition, take a SCUBA class, live on an Indian reservation and learn primitive skills, work in a volunteer program to help others.

Strategies for getting teens interested in other groups include:

1. When a teen tries something new, give plenty of reinforcing feedback.

2. Listen. What does a child mention that suggests interest? Write down three things your child has expressed an interest in lately:

   • _____

   • _____

   • _____

3. Give an event or class as a gift.

4. Invite one of their friends. Bringing a friend from a pre-existing corral provides support when trying something new.

5. Let them make a choice from a list of activities.

6. Have them make a list of activities.

7. Arrange ventures outside the corral at least once every two months. Newspapers and parenting publications often carry calendar sections that list events in the local area.

Gaining confidence in multiple corrals encourages self-esteem that is independent of a single group.

MAGIC KEYS

Uniqueness is the second strut in the self-esteem frame. Teens who feel unique will find ways to express their special abilities.

I frequently work with exceptional teens who, when asked to write down five reasons why they are unique, cannot come up with a single example. Parents, upon hearing that Mary or Toby couldn't come up with anything, may exclaim "But of course they are unique, just look at the way they dance or draw or smile or ..." A child's self-esteem increases from her uniqueness only when she is aware of it. For many kids, it is like having a bicycle locked to a lamp post. Sure, it's there, but unless they have the key, it isn't going to take them anyplace.

Adults carry the *magic key* to that lock. Teens think they must become a glamorous movie star, walk on the moon, or become a star athlete before they can be unique. An adult perspective in this case is an advantage. Learn to recognize the glimmers of uniqueness. Encouraging early signs of uniqueness may even lead to greatness. Consider the following three children. In each case, their parents promoted their special qualities:

Do you know a child who asks a million questions? Albert was such a boy. When his father gave him a compass, he asked many questions about the mysterious force that pulled the needle toward North. His parents were patient with their son's questioning mind. They even encouraged it. Students from the nearby university were regularly invited as dinner guests to share both a meal and ideas. Young Albert Einstein did not formulate $E=MC^2$ as a child, but he did develop an inquisitive nature.

Susan was dissatisfied with her teacher's reasoning. The teacher said that girls needn't learn long division. "But then," she asked, "why do boys need to learn it?" The teacher became irate, "Why, just because they are boys." Most little girls would have stopped there, but Susan found excuses to sit conveniently close to the teacher's desk whenever he was explaining mathematics to the boys. In this way, she mastered long division. When she told her father what she had done, she was anxious about what he would think. Rather than be displeased, he asked her to demonstrate and congratulated her on using her mind. Susan B. Anthony's independent nature was evidenced long before she led the movement that gave women the right to vote in the United States.

Wilbur's parents were supportive of their son's inventive nature. One frigid day, his mother told him to come into the house. Since it was too cold to work on his project in the woodshed, he could work on the dining table and the family would eat in the kitchen. When the contraption of bamboo, rubber bands, and paper was ready to test, the family gathered to watch. It was supposed to fly, but instead it fell to the ground. His father assured him that he would eventually figure out the secret of making it fly. Nurturing that early inventive nature led Wilbur and his brother Orville Wright to fly at Kitty Hawk.

Supporting children's unique qualities makes them feel special. The joy of feeling special and being good at something is often all it takes to motivate a child to move in a particular direction. Take time to write down five unique qualities your child exhibits.

1.
2.
3.
4.
5.

Children's self-esteem benefits only when they are aware of their uniqueness. So how do you make them aware?

One way to make teens aware of their uniqueness is to use a modified form of reinforcing feedback. Remember the five elements in reinforcing feedback: Catch 'em, Immediacy, Positive, Specific, and I-Messages. To ensure that teens are aware of their uniqueness, we add a sixth element to reinforcing feedback, a magic key. The magic key is a key word added after the specific statement. This key word sums up the characteristic you want to promote.

- "Writing a song for a book report, that's CREATIVE."
- "Playing basketball with the big kids took COURAGE."
- "Look at this model. The paint job makes it look like a real starship. That's WORKMANSHIP."

Pronounce the key word in a different tone of voice so that it stands out like a theater billboard surrounded by twinkling lights. The title you assign to a child's actions has a powerful effect on self-image. If a teen hears this key word assigned to her actions a number of times, she incorporates the title into her personality.

Focus on a child's unique qualities with magic key words.

A team approach can be used to reinforce a child's sense of uniqueness. At Deer Crossing, instructors set aside time to discuss campers' positive traits. Primed by these discussions, counselors are on the lookout to catch kids being unique. When they catch a child being unique, the instructors attach a key word to their specific praise. You don't have to run a summer camp to team up looking for the good in kids. A spouse can be your team, or grandmas and grandpas, brothers, sisters, aunts, uncles, or teachers and coaches. Magic keys from multiple sources may be the combination that unlocks a child's special trait.

Using key words takes sensitivity. If you pick every little thing a teen does and use a key word, you lose credibility. "Jon, what an incredible job of tying your shoelaces, that's *GENIUS*." Unwarranted statements like this label adults as unreliable. Use magic keys only when you sincerely believe the action warrants it for the level your child is at.

Use your voice to make a magic key word stand out.

Instructors at Deer Crossing Camp make an effort to find out what the unique characteristics are in children:

> New campers were taking turns telling us where they were from. When it was Bob's turn, he said the minimum. But there was something unique about his voice. Rather than moving on, I commented, "What a wonderfully clear voice. Sounds like an *ACTOR'S VOICE*." He could barely contain his smile.
>
> Over the next four weeks, the instructors learned more about Bob and, as is our philosophy, they created opportunities for him to express his uniqueness. While hiking, one of our instructors asked if Bob knew a ghost story? He didn't. Could he make one up? As they hiked along, Bob made up a story. It was pretty good. The instructor asked if Bob would use his actor's voice to tell the story at campfire.
>
> Even though he felt uncomfortable in front of groups, Bob overcame his stage fright and told his story.

The campers gave him an ovation. Bob had added to his feeling of being unique.

SUPER HERO'S CLOSET

The third piece in our self-esteem framework is the Super Hero's Closet. How it got this title takes a little explanation. As a youngster, my parents included me in a bizarre pastime of theirs (according to my perspective at the time). I would accompany them on the weekend to look at empty houses. Nothing is more boring to a kid than real estate — especially on weekends. I would mope from room to room. My parents, being incredibly perceptive, recognized my mood. They came up with a solution, a stack of super hero comic books. And, in the family Oldsmobile, on the odd Saturday, I made a discovery to rival Einstein's.

Enter my six-year old mind and follow my logic:

I read ten jillion comics. In each, the super hero wears a costume. Why do they hafta' wear costumes? Why couldn't they just wear sneakers, jeans, and tee shirts like the rest of us?

(Then it hit me.) I bet they get their super powers from the costumes.

(This was followed by a quantum leap.) If they get their super powers from costumes, then to be the greatest super hero of all time, you'd hafta' wear a part of each super hero's costume.

This childhood revelation launched a quest. I proceeded to scour toy departments, looking for parts of super heros' costumes — a Superman tee shirt, Batman's cape, etc. I also threw in a few items for good measure, such as The Lone Ranger's mask and Davy Crockett's coonskin cap. It was an incredible outfit, and it resided in a cardboard box in my closet, appropriately labeled — Super Hero's Closet. When I tell this story to teens, I slip into a Batman tee shirt and the Lone Ranger's mask. They look at me suspiciously. Then I tell them I still have a Super Hero's Closet. At this, I detect uncomfortable side glances. But my super hero's wardrobe no longer resides in a closet. It is in my mind. Just as I once collected masks, capes, and other symbols of heroic ability, now I collect true stories of special traits.

Children assemble their personalities from the pieces available to them. To assemble a super-personality, they need examples of real life super-traits, stories in which vague words are transformed into concrete action. Let me take you into my super-traits closet.

The first coat hanger reads Captain Courageous.

Captain Courageous

He was a young boy at summer camp. The diving board fascinated him. He watched the other kids go off, but it was too scary, so he passed on it. Another summer came. Again, the board was too scary. During his third summer, he asked his cabin counselor if he could go off the board. The counselor said he would ask the director. The director thought about it and gave permission.

As the boy came out to the pool deck, he was greeted by the entire camp sitting in the bleachers. When he reached the board, two counselors lifted him from his wheelchair. He was a quadriplegic, paralyzed from the neck down. They carried him to the end of the board. For a moment in time he flew. He had a huge grin as he splashed down into the arms of the waiting lifeguards. The kids in the stands went wild. That day, Captain Courageous shared part of his costume with everyone at this camp for the handicapped.

Wonder Grandma

My Dutch grandmother told me a story that gave me a coat hanger labeled ingenuity. When Indonesia was invaded by the Japanese in World War II, she became a prisoner of war. She managed to smuggle several gold coins into the concentration camp where she was held. Life in the camp was harsh. If the guards discovered anything of value, they would take it. So she wrapped the coins in burlap, making buttons for the front of her burlap bag dress. As the years progressed, she broke the coins into fragments and traded them through the wire fence for the one food item she craved, bell peppers. One of the life-threatening diseases in the camps was scurvy, caused by a lack of vitamin C. It so happens that bell peppers contain more vitamin C than oranges. Her ingenuity helped her survive.

There are real super heros all around us. They wear costumes of honesty, loyalty, humor, perseverance, charity, and calmness. If teens meet these people and attach concrete examples to abstract words, they start their own Super Hero's Closet. Association with people who have special traits adds to self-esteem. Adults can help.

Imagine taking your teen to see where you work (entering another corral). Your boss is a particularly funny guy. He tells a joke in your child's presence and you respond. "You know, Charlie, when you use those different voices, I can almost see the characters in the room, and it really cracks me up." You have just used reinforcing feedback. Feedback highlights an element you feel is involved in humor. Your boss is not the only beneficiary. Your child is now in an environment in which good traits are emphasized. This makes a specific example available to hang in your child's Super Hero's Closet. Feedback benefits more than the recipient.

Let's take the Super Hero's Closet a step further. Introduce your child to exceptional people both living and dead. Living people yes, but dead people?

Famous People — Past And Present

Biographies can introduce teens to famous people, from the present and the past. One obstacle faced by a parent who is trying to encourage a child to read is the sheer number of pages in many biographies. A teen picks up a book with 500 pages and thinks the rest of his life will be devoted to reading this book. Fortunately, publishers have produced many short biographies designed to interest adolescents. Puffin Books has a series, *Women of Our Time*, with biographies about such diverse people as the anthropologist Margaret Mead and comedienne Carol Burnett. Minstrel Books prints the *My Life* series. Each book in this series highlights an individual involved in a unique occupation, such as a dinosaur expert, the creator of *MAD Magazine*, and Alan Bean, the astronaut. Aladdin Books has an excellent series that concentrates on the childhoods of famous Americans, a perspective many adolescents appreciate. Reading biographies helps a child fill his Super Hero's Closet. (See Appendix 1 for a listing of biographies.)

Children have a natural tendency to collect. They collect Nintendo games, baseball cards, stuffed animals, or they want all the books in a Hardy Boys or Nancy Drew Mystery series. Tap into this collector's habit. Get them started on collecting biographies.

An alternate to books is to go the high tech route. Waaaa waaaaaa Booompa Booompaa. Walkman ear muffs — standard issue head gear for teenagers. In the morning, they plug into cassette decks and jam to school on battery power. It's a two-wired umbilicus with stereo access to their brain waves.

Personal cassette decks can be used for more than a Dolby massage of the eardrums. Tapes can introduce teens to people like Charles Darwin, Helen Keller, Bill Cosby, Abraham Lincoln, Lee Iacocca, and Mickey Mantle. What characteristics do these successful individuals share?

There are a variety of ways to encourage listening to biographical tapes:

1. Share your enthusiasm, "Hey, I just listened to this great tape about the Raider's football coach, John Madden. Would you like to borrow it?"

2. Try an exchange, "I'll buy you the *Rad Dudes* cassette, if you'll listen to some tapes I picked out at the library."

3. Put their Walkman at risk, "Let's call it rent. You listen to one tape a week and you keep the cassette player." Note: Let them choose tapes (with redeeming value). This softens the dictator approach.

4. Do you ever go on long trips with your kids? "Geez, kids, we're on our way to New York from California, and I just happen to have a tape on Martin Luther King."

Listen to tapes before giving them to your teen. Does the tape contain thoughts that will benefit your child? Will your child find the tape interesting? If you have a baseball fan, the biography of Mickey Mantle may be of interest. A budding biologist may be inspired by Charles Darwin. A future entrepreneur may enjoy the story of Ray Kroc, the founder of McDonald's.

Some pointers on using tapes to build a Super Hero's Closet:

1. Multiple listenings are more effective. It's easy to listen to some tapes three times and learn something new each time. If a teen likes a particular tape, purchase it for him.

2. Make it a habit to keep tapes in the car. Listen to tapes together during trips and talk about what you have learned.

3. Make it a game. Listen to a tape, and then ask each other questions to see how much information is retained. If competition would spice up the game, keep score. You could even write down questions and make up a game like Trivial Pursuit.

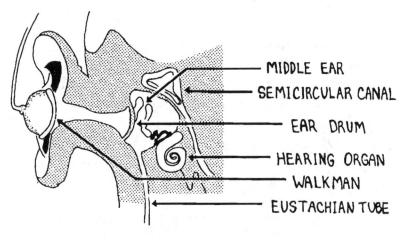

MIDDLE EAR
SEMICIRCULAR CANAL
EAR DRUM
HEARING ORGAN
WALKMAN
EUSTACHIAN TUBE

Anatomy of the teenage ear

By listening to good tapes, a teen is developing a habit used by achievement-oriented adults. Successful individuals know the importance of reinforcing themselves with positive ideas, examples, and stories. If teens are using all those batteries, let's do as a popular commercial says, "Let's energize them." Use those batteries to pump good ideas into their heads along with the good vibes. (See Appendix 2 for a list of tapes teens might enjoy.)

Another high tech method for introducing teens to well-known personalities is through video. Documentaries about Mark Twain, Mother Teresa, and Mahatma Gandhi offer children yet another way to add to their closet of examples. (See Appendix 3.)

A well-stocked Super Hero's Closet helps kids avoid the corral syndrome (see the previous section on belonging). It is like having exceptional imaginary friends. Many famous people put up with embarrassment and overcame tremendous personal odds to fulfill their dreams. These stories inspire the courage needed to visit new groups.

When teens have a well-stocked Super Hero's Closet, parents can help them solve problems in an interesting way. If a teen is challenged by some obstacle, ask the child, "How would _____ (Helen Keller or Benjamin Franklin or Carol Burnett or Joe Montana or Harry Houdini or Rachel Carson) have handled this situation?" This is a variation on the open-ended question covered in Chapter 2. Borrowing from the strategies of successful people, your child has a unique way to solve problems. It's like having access to a group of marvelous mentors.

Use all three mediums — books, tapes, and videos — to make an indelible imprint. If a teen is interested in someone like Einstein, encourage him to read a book, listen to a tape, and watch a video. Give teens a feeling that they really know exceptional people. They then have access to super examples for their Super Hero's Closet.

POWER

We now have three parts of the self-esteem frame welded together: Positive Belonging, Magic Keys, and the Super Hero's

Closet. The fourth and final connecting rod is Power. Power is a sense of control over your destiny. If you feel you can steer the course of your fate, you are more likely to grab the handlebars and do so. This is a tricky ingredient. You often hear of teens who grab the power but not the responsibility. This kind of power is like having a credit card but not having to pay the bill. Start a child early, and they learn that true power involves both control and responsibility.

There are a variety of surprising ways to give teens a sense of power. One way is through chores.

Chore lists are often dominated by the Big Four: wash the dishes, mow the lawn, take out the garbage, and pooper-scooper patrol. Parents admonish teens that such chores teach responsibility.

If you were working for a company, Family Inc., and you knew your major tasks for the next ten years would be "take out the garbage" jobs, how much would this add to your sense of responsibility? What may give a feeling of responsibility to a five-year old is slave labor to a thirteen-year old. Teens aren't stupid. If you want to enhance responsibility through chores, upgrade chores as teens mature. Mature teens need mature chores.

Mrs. Robbins was mowing the lawn. Her sixteen-year old son was busy. Inside the house, he had a stack of cancelled checks to his right. On his left was a variety of bills: utilities, mortgage, phone, car loan coupons, and credit card statements. When he balanced the family budget, he'd write checks for outstanding bills. The stack of checks would then be handed to his mother for her signature. Next month, his mother would handle the checks and he'd be back on the lawn mower.

Mrs. Robbins did not catapult her son from the task of mowing the lawn to sudden fiscal responsibility. Over time, she introduced her child to chores that are progressively more sophisticated. She realized that true power comes in three stages: training, repetition of training to establish consistency, and then handing over responsibility.

To monitor her progress, she uses a checklist. On such a list, a complex task is broken down into bite-sized training chunks. These lists outline concrete goals. The following checklists illustrate the use of this technique.

Monetary Responsibility Checklist

The following list is an example of progressively more sophisticated fiscal chores:

- ❏ Open a savings account
- ❏ Open a checking account (One parent, concerned with too much responsibility too fast, created a make-believe bank. Photocopied checks and bank books were made available to the children. Allowances were deposited in their accounts. To make a withdrawal, the teens wrote checks and received the money from the parent.)
- ❏ Write a check
- ❏ Balance a checkbook
- ❏ Use a credit card
- ❏ Be able to read bills
  - ❏ Credit card statement
  - ❏ Power company bill
  - ❏ Car loan
  - ❏ House mortgage
  - ❏ Medical insurance
- ❏ Understand a loan payment schedule

When chores are used to build a sense of power, remember, if all kids do are pooper-scooper chores expect a pooper-scooper sense of power.

❑ Pay bills

❑ Balance a budget

❑ Fill out an income tax form

On sophisticated chores, children may make mistakes. A parent who gave fiscal responsibility to her son in the form of paying several bills found a late fee in the mail. The child had made an error in calculating the phone bill. Rather than dwell on the mistake, the parent thought in terms of what "outlast" would mean. In the long run, what would most benefit the child? In this case, she turned the mistake into a learning experience. The teen made calls and wrote, explaining the error. It was to no avail, but the teen learned a valuable lesson.

Automotive Responsibility Checklist

When working with a responsibility checklist, repetition is as important as training. Driving a car with a manual transmission one time does not make someone competent. Nor do one shot learning experiences make parents comfortable with giving control to a child. The goal is to repeat experiences over time, with decreasing supervision and increasing consistency.

Here is a possible automotive responsibility checklist:

❑ Add appropriate gas at a self-serve station

❑ Change a tire

❑ Check battery, radiator, brake fluid, windshield washer

❑ Replace fluids

❑ Do basic auto maintenance (e.g., replace a headlight, change oil filter, change spark plugs, flush the radiator, replace a fuse, replace air cleaner element, change a wiper blade)

❑ Take a car in for service, describe the problem, read the contract, and limit payments for work done

❑ Practice driving

❑ Read an auto insurance policy and understand the coverage

How often should something be repeated? If you really had a flat tire, would you feel comfortable with your child making the change — without watching over her shoulder? If you answer yes, then your child has probably done enough repetitions to be consistent. Now the teen has earned responsibility.

A Cooking Responsibility Checklist

In the quest for responsibility, kids can be discouraged by parents. One twelve-year old said, "My Mom doesn't want me to handle things in the kitchen. She's afraid I might ruin the meat for dinner or make a mess." It's important for parents to look beyond possible temporary inconvenience. (Remember: Our Purpose Is Not To Win, It Is To Outlast.) Good training minimizes problems. You will also have to repeat training on complex tasks until the child becomes proficient. Is an occasional messy kitchen worth a gain in self-confidence and responsibility?

Being able to feed yourself is one of the most basic responsibilities:

❑ Prepare dessert (e.g., start with something like Jello and progress up to the difficulty of a pie)

❑ Prepare individual items in a meal (e.g., cook meat, prepare salad, cook vegetables)

❑ Prepare full meal

❑ Prepare a meal from a cookbook

❑ Purchase food

    ❑ How to pick fruits and vegetables

    ❑ How to choose a cut of meat

    ❑ How to figure out the best price for an item at the supermarket

❑ Prepare a nutritionally balanced menu and cook a full day of meals

❑ Prepare a week's menus, do the shopping, and prepare all meals

The twelve-year old mentioned above convinced her mother to let her cook. After several weeks of training, the child prepared a full spaghetti dinner without assistance. The mother told me that her daughter had a smile from ear to ear when she served this meal. The child's self-confidence in this area had gone up several notches.

If you are willing to upgrade a child's level of chores, you may also have to become more democratic in dealing with the child. This may entail doing some lower level tasks yourself. For instance, if your daughter makes dinner, maybe you wash the dishes. If your daughter does the shopping, maybe you mow the lawn. This creates a sense of equality, responsibility goes up a notch, and children have a greater appreciation for what parents provide. In the first chapter, it was pointed out that experience is often the most expedient method of getting across your point. Chores, like cooking dinner, expand your child's viewpoint.

A Safety Responsibility Checklist

A basic first aid class makes teens more reliable babysitters. Parents have greater confidence in a teen who recognizes hazards and who knows how to respond to an accident.

❑ Can he treat a wound in a sterile fashion?

❑ Know how to stop major bleeding?

❑ Know what to do if a person has a broken limb?

❑ Know what to do if someone is choking?

❑ Know how to administer cardiopulmonary resuscitation (CPR)?

❑ For children around the water, consider a basic lifeguarding class.

(American Red Cross offers first aid and lifeguard courses)

Transportation Responsibility Checklist

Teens need to get around. Part of their checklist might include:

❑ Use a street map to navigate to five points they have never visited

❑ Use public transportation

❑ Make reservations for accommodations on a trip

❑ Make reservations for travel by plane, train, bus, or boat

A thirteen-year old in one of my leadership training programs got permission to plan a family ski trip. She made reservations at a motel, booked plane tickets, and located several restaurants for meals. After the trip she said, "It really made me feel like an important member of the family."

Household Maintenance Responsibility Checklist

Living in a house offers all kinds of responsible chores:

❑ Replace light bulbs with appropriate wattage

❑ Replace a fuse or reset a circuit breaker

❑ Relight the pilot on a furnace or water heater

❑ Drain a water heater

❑ Paint a room

❑ Unplug a drain

❑ Unplug a toilet

❑ Set a thermostat

❑ Replace and clean furnace and air conditioner filters

❑ Defrost a freezer

❑ Clean the stove and oven

❑ Make a straight saw cut

❑ Drill a hole

❑ Drive a nail

❑ Hang a picture frame

❑ Put up a shelf

❑ Tighten a bolt

❑ Sharpen a knife

Fred, a parent in one of my workshops, remembered when he was ten and his father asked him to repair a broken gate. His Dad had trained him how to use tools, but this was the first time his father had given him a project without any supervision. Fred said he never forgot the feeling of importance he got from fixing that gate. Every time he walked through the repaired gate, he felt a sense of accomplishment. Over the years, he was given more responsibility. Fred said that these childhood experiences gave him the self-confidence that eventually enabled him to build his home.

Check the preceding lists. What tasks have you trained your child in? Has she done sufficient repetitions that you would feel confident in handing over the task? Training a child in advanced chores is an advanced skill for adults. Having a checklist, such as in the previous examples, encourages consistency. If a teen sees continuing progress on such a list, it bolsters self-confidence. It also gives teens a sense of control over their destiny.

(For an example of an extensive list used in training children toward adult skills, check *Survival Kit for Parents of Teenagers* by David Melton, Saint Martin's Press, New York, 1979. An extensive skills checklist starts on page 298.)

A Positive Sense of Belonging, Magic Keys, Super Hero's Closet, and Power make up the four struts in a self-esteem frame. Welding these four elements into a self-esteem frame strengthens an adult's ability to motivate. Kids raised in this kind of environment will reach their full potential, and develop the self-confidence necessary to become self-motivated. How can you motivate yourself to make sure these four elements are included in your child's growth? One way is to keep a self-esteem calendar.

SELF-ESTEEM CALENDAR

Instructors at Deer Crossing Camp get self-esteem calendars every two weeks. These are simple wall calendars with an empty box for each day. At the end of every day, instructors fill the calendar boxes with concrete examples of what they have done to build camper self-esteem. Snip out the calendar at the end of this chapter and give it a try.

Post the calendar on your private bathroom mirror. If it is right at tooth-brushing or hair-combing level, it will be hard to ignore. Tie a string to a pencil and tape it to the calendar. This calendar is going to serve as a daily diary of how you contribute to self-esteem in the four categories.

Before bed each night, look at the calendar. Think back through the day to a specific instance of *reinforcing feedback* given to a child. Write it down. Your goal is to have an example of feedback recorded under each day. At the end of a week, you will have seven examples.

The second item to track on the calendar is a child's uniqueness. If you caught a child being special, write down the *magic key word* you used to make her aware of her uniqueness.

Third, make plans on the calendar to pick up something for the *Super Hero's Closet.* Maybe you will pick up several biographical tapes from the library on Saturday. Next Tuesday, plan on going to the video store to see if they have documentaries on exceptional people. Maybe schedule a trip to the bookstore to order several biographies your teen would be interested in.

Finally, in the area of *power*, decide what advanced chores you can teach your child. List on the calendar when he will start this training. Maybe he will make dessert this week or learn how to cook spaghetti.

The calendar symbolizes commitment and consistency in raising a child's self-esteem. Calendars enable us to plot our progress and see areas where imbalance is occurring — maybe you are solid on feedback but thin on power, or maybe you are good with *key words,* but the *Super Hero's Closet* needs more hangers. The calendar checks that all four parts in a self-esteem frame are being worked on. If each calendar box contains a motivational example at the end of the week, reward yourself. Go out to dinner and take in a movie.

If you expect kids to grow to their full physical stature, a balanced nutritional diet containing proteins, carbohydrates, vitamins, and minerals is necessary. Stunted children are the result of leaving vital elements out of their nutrition. In earlier times, people did not understand the principle of balanced foods. Feudal Japan is a prime example. In early Japan much of the populace subsisted on rice. Rice by itself lacks important vitamins. Children raised on such a diet are stunted. It is interesting to note that Japanese who moved to the United States in the early 1800's often conceived children who towered over the parents. This growth spurt is attributed to the adoption of a new diet in their new home. This balanced diet enabled children to grow to their full potential.

Like nutrition, self-esteem is composed of four elements. A balanced self-esteem diet contains: positive belonging, magic keys, Super Hero's Closet, and power. When all four elements are present, children have the greatest chance of reaching their full potential.

SELF-ESTEEM SUMMARY

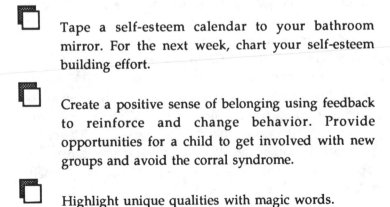

Tape a self-esteem calendar to your bathroom mirror. For the next week, chart your self-esteem building effort.

Create a positive sense of belonging using feedback to reinforce and change behavior. Provide opportunities for a child to get involved with new groups and avoid the corral syndrome.

Highlight unique qualities with magic words.

☐ Add to a teen's Super Hero's Closet.

    a. Introduce children to special people.

    b. Provide autobiographical books, cassettes, and videos.

☐ Increase a teen's sense of power by upgrading chores.

Keep a self-esteem calendar to keep track of your efforts at providing a balanced self-esteem diet.

Sun	Mon	Tues	Wed	Thurs	Fri	Sat

THE GOAL STEERING SYSTEM AND WHEELS

Teaching Teens To Motivate Themselves

Riding along on our motivational bicycle, we come upon a bicycle race.

It is immediately clear that of the three riders in the race, two are at a disadvantage. One is handicapped by a blindfold. His chances are slim. The second cyclist has a better chance. No blindfold obscures his view of the destination, but his handlebars are missing. It looks like he is in for an uncertain ride. The third rider is the most likely to arrive at her destination. She sees where she is going and has handlebars to steer with.

Teens want to be successful. The problem for many of them is they don't know how to get started. It is like wanting to reach a destination but being blindfolded or lacking handlebars to steer in that direction. This chapter is about helping teens establish a clear destination and giving them a simple steering system to get there.

The system about to be described will help teens develop the self-motivational trait of *goal steering*. Goal steering has five easy steps:

1. Write down goals in a dream book.
2. Be specific about these goals.
3. Use a plus and minus chart to decide if a goal is worthwhile.
4. Ask the same questions a reporter would ask to map out your goal.
5. Chart progress on a calendar.

WRITE DOWN GOALS IN A DREAM BOOK

Reaching a destination while wearing a blindfold is difficult. Teens who have a clear vision of their destination have a better chance of arriving. This is the purpose of a dream book — to clarify goals.

A dream book is simply a bound book with blank pages, similar to a diary. In this book, teens record aspirations. Any goal, no matter how far-fetched, is included in the book.

Writing down goals is the beginning step for turning dreams into reality. John Goddard, a world famous explorer, is a strong believer in the power of writing down your goals:

Goddard relates, "At fifteen, I was aware that many adults wished they could live their lives over. They wait and wait for their ships to come in. In the meantime, their piers collapse. I thought if I could crystallize my ambitions and start working on them early, life wouldn't pass me by. It's like building a raft and rowing out to meet your ship."

Goddard started building his raft in the form of a remarkable list — he calls it his "life list." At fifteen, he took a sheet of legal paper and wrote out 127 goals. These goals included: type 50 words per minute (#81), visit a movie studio (#119), become an Eagle Scout (#73), and hold breath underwater for two and a half minutes (#78). Other goals were more challenging: read the entire Encyclopedia Britannica (#109), milk a poisonous snake (#117), climb Mt. Kilimanjaro and the Matterhorn (#25 and #30), learn to speak French, Spanish, and Arabic (#104), visit every country in the world (#38), land a plane on an aircraft carrier (#75), ride an elephant, camel, ostrich, and bronco (#77), and explore the Nile and Congo Rivers (#1 and #3). At 67 years of age, John Goddard has accomplished 108 of his original 127 goals. He has been called the real Indiana Jones.[*]

Writing goals in a dream book encourages teens to think about where they are going in life. If they reply, "Oh, I don't want to write it down because I might change my mind," remind them that paper isn't concrete. The dream book is a way for teens to discover what is important to them. It helps narrow down the infinite possibilities. It can become a personal catalog of goals. Teens who travel the furthest often have a destination.

---

[*] You and your teen might enjoy John Goddard's book, *Kayaks Down the Nile*, an account of the first complete descent of the Nile River. It is a book for the Super Hero's Closet. To obtain a copy, write to John Goddard at 4224 Beulah Drive, La Canada, California 91011.

For balance, three types of dreams should be included in the dream book: Things (T), Experiences (E), and Characteristics (C). This will make it a high *TEC* dream book (please excuse the pun). *Things* might include getting a remote control car, a mountain bike, a gold necklace, or a Walkman. *Experiences* could be going to the Senior Prom, visiting another state, or taking a modeling class. *Characteristics* represent incorporation of new traits into one's personality, such as improving your memory for names, showing greater tolerance, or learning to use reinforcing feedback. A balance of big and small goals should be entered in the book.

Date and number the entries. This makes the book more interesting to refer to as the years go on.

From the dream books of several teenagers:

1. Learn to SCUBA dive. (E)
2. Get along better with my brother and sister. (C)
3. Go to college in Australia. (E)
4. Get in touch with six friends from my old high school. (E)
5. Get a CD player. (T)
6. Place first in a piano competition. (E)
7. Become a pilot. (C)
8. Fight less at school. (C)
9. Read two books on Einstein. (E)
10. Ask questions in English class without feeling like a dummy. (C)
11. High jump 4 feet 6 inches. (E)
12. Lose eleven pounds. (C)
13. Be nicer. (C)
14. Do 30 consecutive kicks on a hacky sack. (C)
15. Get a Mercedes 300 SL. (T)

Teens start a dream book by writing out ten or more ambitions. They keep the book in an accessible place, such as a nightstand near their bed. Additional goals are added as the years go on.

BE SPECIFIC ABOUT GOALS

A hazy goal is like peddling toward a destination in dense fog.

If a teenager says, "I want to be rich," I hand them a nickel and say, "You're richer. What's your next goal?"

They sputter, "A nickel isn't what I meant by rich."

"Well, how rich do you want to be? A thousand dollars, ten thousand, a million? Will that be in cash, securities, gold bullion, property, rare antiques?"

Teens should define their destinations the best they can before writing them down.

Another hazy goal that teenagers often grump about is, "I want my parents off my back." Does this mean parents should quit bugging teens about homework? Maybe they want their parents to sign over the deed to the house and move? Or do they simply want more time on the telephone?

Be specific about destinations. To practice being specific, look at the list of goals on page 102. Some of these dreams are vague. Circle ambiguous goals, and see if you can bring a fuzzy goal into sharp focus by rewriting it. For example, goal number seven, *Become a pilot*, could be made more specific by changing it to, "Get a pilot's license to fly a Cessna." Goal thirteen, *Be nicer*, would be more precise if it was changed to, "Smile at least five times a day, and use reinforcing feedback twice a day to classmates." Reworded, these dreams become clearer destinations which are easier to steer towards. See if you can improve goals two, eight, and ten.

Three more steps enable teens not only to see their destination but give them handlebars to steer in that direction.

USE A PLUS AND MINUS CHART TO DETERMINE IF A GOAL IS WORTHWHILE

Having destinations is not enough. Now a decision must be made as to which routes to travel. What are you willing to do to make the trip? Will you sacrifice TV time for study time, give up trips to the refrigerator to avoid walks to the scale, or exchange lazy weekends for a busy job at McDonald's? The third step in the Goal Steering System is to use a *Plus and Minus Chart*. The plus and minus chart helps teens decide whether it is worthwhile to pedal to a particular destination. This is a judgment call that can only be made by the cyclist.

Take a sheet of paper. Draw a vertical line down the center of the page. Label one column "plus" and the other "minus." In the plus column, list all the positive benefits that would be obtained by going after this goal. In the minus column, list all the drawbacks of going after the goal. Benjamin Franklin used a similar technique whenever he was trying to make a decision. A list is a concrete way of deciding whether commitment is worthwhile.

Worthwhile is a subjective decision. It is not a matter of adding up the columns and going with the one that has the most. When comparing the plus and minus columns, there may be only one item on the plus side, but that single positive may outweigh all the negatives. The pleasure a teen anticipates from learning to play the piano may offset all the negatives of having to give up time with friends, less time for homework, and less time for play. Or there may be dozens of things on the plus side and only a few in the negative column. A child who sees many advantages in earning money from a job after school may drop the goal because of a single item in the negative column — he would have to give up after-school sports. The decision is the teen's.

The plus and minus chart assists teens in making decisions. It helps them avoid being caught in the loop of being so afraid to commit to anything that they end up with nothing.

TO MAP OUT A GOAL, ASK THE SAME QUESTIONS A REPORTER WOULD ASK

The fourth step in the Goal Steering System consists of *asking questions* and finding answers. This section gives teens a firm grip on steering toward goals.

Teens start by asking questions — the same questions a reporter would ask: Who, What, Where, When, and How.

Who: do I need help from, need to contact, need to convince ...

What: resources do I need, books, education, money ...

Where: can I do it, get what I need ...

When: will I do it ...

How: will I get the time, money, confidence ...

For instance, in one of my leadership classes, fourteen-year old Mike wanted to improve his Spanish grade from a C to a B. His goal steering outline follows:

"**Who** can help me decide what to study?"

Answer: My Spanish teacher, and maybe a friend who has taken the course before.

"**What** will I study?"

Answer: My Spanish teacher suggested practicing the dialogs in Chapters 11 and 12. My friend is going to let me borrow the flashcards he used last quarter.

"Where will I study to get the most benefit?"

Answer: Study hall is too noisy and home has too many distractions. The library seems like the best choice.

"When will I study?"

Answer: After dinner, I'll go to the library.

"How much time should I study?"

Answer: My teacher says it will take about an hour a night. I'll study from 6:00 to 7:00.

Just as he kept track of his goals in a dream book, Mike wrote down his questions and answers in a goal binder. The process of writing down questions and answers enabled him to visualize the strategy for reaching a goal. Every time a question was asked and answered, he traveled closer to attainment of his goal.

Parents may occasionally help with questions but should avoid giving answers. Children taught to think in this manner become solution-oriented. If there is an obstacle, the child asks another question and searches for the answer. This will steer teens over, under, around, or through obstacles.

In goal steering workshops, students start with a short-range goal that can be accomplished in two to four weeks. Teens have chosen goals such as: juggle three balls for 30 seconds, do ten pull-ups, work on math problems at the end of the chapter for one hour every night for a month, and read two books on Einstein. If a 30-day commitment seems too long, start with goals that can be done in a single day. Short goals enable the adult motivator to give swift feedback, which is sometimes necessary to reinforce goal-oriented behavior. Simple one day goals could be: cook cinnamon swirl muffins, read a short biography, learn ten words in French, go fishing for bass, learn to tie a bowline knot, buy a dream book — anything that hasn't been done before but where there is an interest.

Beginners must start with attainable goals. If a fifteen-year old selects a massive goal such as "I want to go to college," urge her to break it down into manageable 30-day pieces. Ordering catalogs from three different colleges would be a good start. Another possibility would be to visit two nearby college campuses and arrange to speak with a counselor. In the early stages of using the Goal Steering System, the student must be successful. Success encourages a goal steering mentality.

CHART PROGRESS ON A CALENDAR

The final step in the Goal Steering System is periodic review of progress. Returning to the goal binder weekly, the teen checks that he has adequately answered his questions. He also anticipates any other questions that may help him toward his goal. Posting a conspicuous calendar that charts progress keeps teens on track. This calendar is similar to the self-esteem calendar described in the previous chapter.

On the calendar, teens write down dates to review their progress, target dates for finding answers, and accomplishments. A teen in one of my programs had the goal of shaving 30 seconds off her mile run. Her review calendar logged the days she ran and times for those runs. She also listed appointments with a coach to answer questions about nutrition as well as meetings with other runners who could answer questions about technique. The calendar kept her on track and she improved her mile time by more than 30 seconds.

When reviewing progress with a teen, use reinforcing feedback (see Chapter 3) to encourage these goal-oriented steps. At first, a weekly review is beneficial. As skill develops, a monthly review is sufficient. Eventually teens should learn to do their review without supervision.

After accomplishing a 30-day goal, the teen should return to his dream book to date and star the accomplished goal. The dream book becomes part of a child's Super Hero's Closet, serving as a reminder of past successes. It also encourages teens to try more difficult goals.

> In one of my classes, students challenged me to steer toward one of my goals. Inspired by cartoonist Gary Larson's *The Far Side*, I had listed a goal in my dream book, "sell a cartoon to a national magazine." My students asked me to turn this dream into reality. Even though I have no formal art background, I accepted the challenge.
>
> I set up a plus and minus chart and decided it was worthwhile.
>
> Then came the reporter's questions. Some of my questions were: How will I learn to draw cartoons? Answer: Study Gary Larson's books and those of other famous cartoonists. Who will I sell to? Answer: Pick up copy of *Artist's Market* ... and so on.
>
> Eventually I set aside several weeks and did nothing but draw until the wee hours of the morning. Some cartoons looked plausible. Six months later, my first cartoons were published. I have since sold cartoons to a variety of publications, including *The Bay Area Parent, Black Belt Magazine, COMDEX, Sources, SKI Magazine,* and *The San Francisco Chronicle.*

To develop a goal steering mentality, teens should practice with the system for one year. Every month they pick a goal that can be accomplished in 30 days. The power of the system lies in the concrete way in which teens see dreams transformed into reality. The dream book and goal binder are tangible representations of the goal-setting process. A dream book filled with stars of accomplishment becomes a symbol of the ability to turn dreams into reality. Remember how important it is for a child's self-esteem to have a sense of power or control over her destiny? Having a strategy for turning dreams into reality builds that power.

An alternative to a goal binder is to take a sheet of computer paper as long as the child is tall. Attach the paper to the door of her room. Do the question and answer format on this sheet. Its high profile reminds kids to think in terms of goal-setting. When the 30-day goal is complete, store the computer paper in a goal binder and stick a new sheet on the wall.

ROLLING TOWARD ADULTHOOD

Sometimes teens need help in deciding where they might set goals.

What follows is a quiz. Originally this quiz determined if adults have a balanced lifestyle. A group of young people helped modify questions on the adult test so that it would be appropriate for teens. This quiz is a simple way of assessing whether a teen is developing balance in life. It offers a graphic representation of areas that need pumping up.

Pretend to be your child and answer questions from his viewpoint. Then let your teen take the same test. Often parental perceptions differ dramatically from the child's viewpoint. This information alone is helpful. An understanding of where your teen is coming from may help you figure out where he is going. (**Caution:** Do not give the impression of failure if the results do not meet your expectations. This is a tool to point out areas you may want to help your child grow in.)

A Set Of Wheels For Your Teenager

When answering the following questions, teens should rate themselves from 1 to 10 (10 is high). For example, question #1 asks teens if they have a variety of friends. If they have a couple of friends on the volleyball team, one in the electronics club, several in Scouts, several they go to the mall with, a bunch in the drama club, a few kids on their block, and a pen pal overseas, they give themselves a 10. On the other hand, if all their friends consist of the group they hang out with at the mall, they give themselves a 1 or 2. (Questions 8, 16 and 24 are blank. These blanks are explained in the wheel chart.)

•   •   •   •   •

Rolling Toward Adulthood Quiz

____ 1.	I have a variety of close friends.
____ 2.	I care about myself.
____ 3.	I exercise vigorously three times a week for an hour each time.
____ 4.	I spend quality time with my family.
____ 5.	I have a bank account that I add to regularly.
____ 6.	I have seriously considered what I want for a career.
____ 7.	I do more than just enough to get by at school.
____ 8.	
____ 9.	I have friends whose goals and ideals I respect.
____ 10.	I like to express my ideas.
____ 11.	I eat nutritious, well-balanced meals.
____ 12.	I like to talk with family members.
____ 13.	I have a part-time job to make spending money.
____ 14.	I have goals and regularly invest time in them.
____ 15.	I spend at least 1-1/2 hours every night on homework.
____ 16.	
____ 17.	I enjoy meeting new people at parties and group events.
____ 18.	I feel involved in decisions that affect my life.
____ 19.	I avoid doing things that are bad for my health.
____ 20.	I am responsible and help around the house.
____ 21.	I appreciate and care for things my parents give me.
____ 22.	I complete what I start.
____ 23.	I'm involved in extracurricular school activities.
____ 24.	

How Well Are They Rolling Toward Adulthood?

Now write the scores you gave under the appropriate headings. For example, if you gave your teen five points for #1, you will find #1 under the category "social." After you have transferred all the scores, total the points in each category.

Social	Self-Esteem	Physical	Family
1.	2.	3.	4.
9.	10.	11.	12.
17.	18.	19.	20.
Total	Total	Total	Total

Money-Sense	Goal-Setting	School	Open Spoke*
5.	6.	7.	8.
13.	14.	15.	16.
21.	22.	23.	24.
Total	Total	Total	Total

---

* The "open spoke" is an opportunity for parents to include a category they consider important for the development of their teen, such as moral, spiritual, creative, etc. The parent should make up questions for #8, #16, and #24 which point out attainment of the quality in that category. As an example, for creativity you might use the following statements: Once a week I imagine different ways of doing things. This year I explored ten new places I'd never been to before. I spend several hours a week being creative, such as drawing, composing music, inventing.

Now go to the Teen Success Wheel. Take the total number of points scored in each category and put a dot on the line below the title of the area. When you have plotted all eight points, connect the dots to get a visual representation of the shape and size of your wheel.

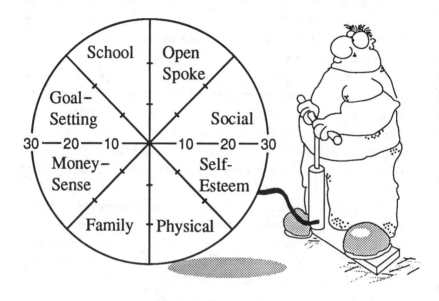

Teen Success Wheel

Many teens ride around on flat tires. These tires represent their preparation for adulthood. When flat or under-inflated, these wheels make for a bumpy ride down the road of life. Teens are often strong in one area on the wheel. For instance, school may be the overriding influence in a teen's life. Teens can be so focused on grades that they don't see the full picture. It's the cliche of the "A" student who ends up flunking life as an adult. The purpose of this test is to point out areas that need pumping up. Fully integrated and happy adults often have a balance. This balance doesn't happen magically but is something that is developed, often in the teen years. How well will your child roll down the path toward adulthood?

An Opportunity Fable

No one understood Sondra. Here it was high noon, the heat-cracked ground sizzled, and she was nowhere to be found. Toby looked at the others crouched in the shade of the giant mushroom rock. Everyone knew there was only one reason to venture into the open. That reason was rain. When it came, everyone would grab their cup and poke it out from under the rock to catch a few glistening drops. When the cloudburst had passed, they would pull back into the shade like a thousand tortoise heads withdrawing under their rock shell. Toby never caught more than a few precious beads of water. But Sondra was his sister, and she shared with him.

Sondra's cup was always full. Yet he had never seen her scramble desperately to the overhang with her cup. In fact, he could not remember seeing her catch drops with the others. Everyone said Sondra was blessed by the gods. Only Toby knew different, today he would discover her secret.

"You look like a dancing lizard," said Sondra.

"Darn it Sondra, the sand's hot. Can't we go another time, maybe when I'm older?"

Sondra scowled. "You're beginning to sound like the others. How old do you have to be? Like Duma? He's 60 summers, and his throat is as parched as the sand we stand on. I tried to share with the others and all they say is, I'm lucky or blessed or more fortunate. It's easier for them to think I possess magic."

Toby had little time to think as his sister turned and walked away. He looked longingly at the shade of the mushroom rock, then back to Sondra.

"Wait for me, Sondra."

The way was not easy. Toby had never known such a strong thirst. At one point, he was ready to give up. Then Sondra stopped: "There is my magic."

Toby stared at the strange thing before him. It was similar to the mushroom rock, but the top was flat and the sides angled up offering little shade. Five stone steps led to the top. Sondra scrambled up. She motioned for Toby to follow. At the top, he teetered on the edge, looking down into the strange hollow rock.

"Careful, don't fall in." Sondra put a steadying arm around Toby.

"How did the rock get this way?"

Sondra looked very proud. "I built the steps and then used a stone to chip away the rock."

"But, why?"

Sondra looked up. "Quick, get down and you will understand." They scrambled down the steps. A large cloud was passing over.

"Give me your cup." Sondra held it near a hole in the pedestal. As the rain fell, Toby watched in stunned amazement. Water began to gush from the hole into his cup. He had never seen so much water.

"Sondra, what is this wonderful thing?"

"I call it a funnel."

"But we have to tell the others about this magic."

Sondra looked knowingly at her brother. "You may get them to dream of a full cup, but the magic is getting them to build an empty funnel."

•   •   •   •   •

GOAL STEERING SUMMARY

The steps teens can take to turn their dreams into reality.

5

THE NEED PEDALS

Persuading Without Pushing — Tapping Into The Six Driving Forces Behind Teen Behavior

Do you ever feel that motivation is like riding a tandem bicycle with only one set of pedals? You're in the front pedaling away while the child sits passively on the rear seat, legs dangling in the air.

If you stop pedaling, the bike comes to a halt. "Tommy, haven't you started your homework yet?" "Denise, for the millionth time, make your bed." "Kim, you really should go out with other people." "Lyle, you spent all the money on a computer game? Haven't we taught you anything about saving?"

Why are teens so obstinate? Their stubbornness is often because adults fail to appreciate a simple principle:

> People are motivated to meet their needs.

Teens are people. If you want children to be self-propelled, find out what their needs are. These needs are their pedals. Teens spend $120 on tennis shoes, not because they desire footwear, but because they need prestige. Children frequent fast food places, not because they want poor nutrition, but because they need to spend as little as possible. A student disrupts a class with his antics not because he craves punishment, but because he needs attention.

A successful motivator learns to meet other people's needs. Extolling the aerobic benefits of folk dancing to a teen may elicit yawns, but when you mention that the opposite gender outnumbers him four to one, he feels rhythm. A teen thinks dust adds character to the family car until Dad explains that weekend use depends on flying elbows and polishing wax. A teen's feet are blocks of ice, and her mother wants her to wear a hat that makes her look like Goofy — no interest — until Mom mentions that it's common knowledge that feet stay warmer when you wear a hat. Hellooooo, Goofy (granted, her feet will probably have to be close to frostbite before she will be willing to look like Goofy).

> A wise merchant offers tea to a thirsty man.
> A foolish shopkeeper offers salted fish.

Meeting another's needs and at the same time meeting your needs is a satisfying way to influence. Both people get what they want. An added benefit of this technique is that it nurtures self-propelled kids, teens who don't need constant goading. To accomplish this type of motivation, you have to figure out the child's needs, determine your needs, and link the two together.

Needs fall into six categories: survival, avoidance, pleasure, belonging, achievement, and power. Each need is like a set of pedals, pedals that persuade teens to do their own pedaling.

Children give both verbal and non-verbal clues as to which needs motivate them. For example, if a teen displays excessive consciousness about her clothing matching her friends' wardrobes, it may show a strong need to belong. Staying up late hours and working hard on a science fair project may demonstrate a need to achieve. Verbal clues sometimes require deciphering. A teen who says, "Dancing is for geeks," may be expressing a need to avoid social situations he feels ill-prepared for. If a child says, "All I am is a dishwasher and garbageperson around here," she may be expressing a need for more power or control over her environment. To unscramble verbal clues, use the reflective listening technique described in Chapter 2. Reflective listening gives insight into which motivational need is being expressed.

Adults must also define their needs. For example, when Mom requires her son to make his bed every morning, what is the motivation? Why is a neat bed important? Maybe there is a need for the child to respond to commands — a need for power. Maybe the parent equates a neat bed with good parenting practice — achievement. Maybe a neat house gives the parent a sense of organization — pleasure. If you discover that your need is different from your child's, search for a way to link your need to your child's need.

Let's take a look at each need category and see how it can be used to encourage new behavior. Again, the six categories are: Survival, Avoidance, Pleasure, Belonging, Achievement, and Power.

SURVIVAL

Survival is the first set of pedals. Physiological requirements such as air, water, food, and warmth represent a major need category. Imagine someone holding your head underwater. You are not interested in money, fame, or Hershey Bars. You are focused on one need — air. I am not suggesting you hold teens' heads underwater to get your way, although sometimes it is tempting. There are positive ways to link behavioral changes to basic needs.

Our society, with its technological bubble packaging and safeguards, meets the subsistence needs of most teens. An effort must be made to set up a survival situation. Let's consider an example.

Programs conducted under wilderness conditions have long been used to motivate behavioral changes. Wilderness survival promotes responsibility, teamwork, resourcefulness, and respect. If the only person who feeds you is yourself, you quickly learn *responsibility*. A group without sleeping bags, facing a cold night in the woods, appreciates the importance of efficient *teamwork* in preparing a campsite. A hungry student standing on a stream bank watches fish swim by and shows *resourcefulness* in fabricating a spear or unraveling a tee shirt for fishing line. Survival conditions encourage students to extend *respect* toward the teacher who is sharing knowledge. Note that in each case a basic subsistence requirement fosters the desired behavior.

A family camping trip is not as intense as a wilderness survival experience, but it can be an excellent environment in which to motivate behavioral changes. On a camping trip, responsibility can be taught by having children set up their tents, prepare their meals, and lead the way down the trail.

How can a parent use the survival need in the home?

A parent in one of my workshops was constantly chasing after her son to make sure he didn't forget his lunch bag. After analyzing the situation, the parent decided she had an achievement need — she wanted to improve her son's memory. The recommendation was to let Mother Nature take over. Forgetting lunch several days in a row was all it took to improve his memory.

Let's say you have another achievement need. You want your fifteen-year old daughter to be more self-reliant. Arrange to leave for the weekend. She has to cook her meals while you are away. Your child is motivated to feed herself; you also satisfy your achievement need by making her more self-reliant.

AVOIDANCE

The next need category is avoidance. The advertising media makes extensive use of this incentive. Commercials induce us to buy aspirin, cough suppressants, and Alka-Seltzer to avoid discomfort. Dismembered crash test dummies talk to us on television and tell us to use seatbelts to avoid their predicament. People spray Ban and gargle Listerine to avoid social unacceptability. Families purchase houses in safe neighborhoods to avoid crime. We are sold many products and ideas based on avoiding problems.

Some parents comment that avoidance is not as powerful a motivational tool as they would like it to be. This may be because parents use only half the avoidance pedal.

The first half of the avoidance pedal is rationality. When trying to convince a teen to avoid something, it is customary to explain the consequences of an action. Logic is a good start, but it is not the place to stop. Teens are also heavily influenced by how they "feel." The second half of the avoidance pedal is to convince their emotions. For example, teens are intelligent enough to understand the incompatibility of drinking and driving. Yet, some teens ignore the rational evidence. They understand, but it doesn't change their behavior. Realizing the importance of the emotional ingredient, school districts have included a strong emotional message in programs designed to deter drinking and driving. Wrecked cars in which drunk drivers died have been towed to campuses. In some cases, the deceased drivers had been students at the school. The twisted wreckage is a harsh reality. Friends could only cry when they saw the crushed metal. A combination of logic and emotion resulted in lowering the incidence of drinking and driving at these schools.

Schools have incorporated similar approaches in response to drugs. Students learn not only the facts but visit rehabilitation clinics to talk with teen substance abusers. When teens talk to someone their age, who has obviously been "wasted" by drugs, any misconceptions about the glamour of drugs are soon dispelled.

Talking to a quadriplegic about his life after a motorcycle accident is a more powerful motivator than quoting statistics on wearing a helmet. *The effectiveness of avoidance depends on both brain and heart involvement.*

(**Caution:** There is a dark side to using avoidance as a motivational tool. Continual use creates fear-motivated teens. They are always moving away from things and concentrating on what they don't want to have happen. Focusing on what you don't want leaves less time for concentrating on what you do want. This reduces children's chances for success. Avoidance, like salt, should be used sparingly.)

PLEASURE

Pleasure is a motivational pedal everyone is familiar with. But it is the Silly Putty of needs. You can twist it, roll it, and mold it into a variety of shapes, a different form for each person. Pleasure is not a constant. Determining what gives pleasure requires insight. Some people get pleasure from dancing, being creative, whistling, chewing gum, learning, playing with a Rubik's cube, meditating, attending a concert, working, and jogging. Other individuals may not find some of these activities pleasurable. Pleasure is personal, like fingerprints.

When a child associates pleasure with an activity, perceptive adults find ways to attach that pleasure to other activities they want to promote. For instance, say a teacher has a teen bored to tears by physics, but discovers that the student is an avid surfer. The wise teacher finds a relation between wave phenomenon and surfing.

- Parents have long known that it is easier to get kids to read things they enjoy. Teachers have resorted to comic books to encourage non-readers. Books that contain dinosaurs are more interesting than *Jack and Jill*. A reluctant reader, thrilled by adventure, may be absorbed by the *National Geographic* account of a teenager who sailed solo around the world. This young sailor's story (*The Dove*) is heavy on pictures and light on words. If a boy is car crazy, get him an automotive manual. If a girl loves art, get her a subscription to an art magazine.

- Poetry is a pain for most teens. You can shift to a pleasure perspective by having teens study a popular musician's songs or have them write their own song. One creative teacher had students bring musical instruments and turn poems into music.

- If teens enjoy music and you want them to exercise, do aerobics to music (someone came up with this idea and started the aerobic dance craze — turn off the music and watch the interest drop).

- If teens enjoy television, and you want to promote history, show clips of events and period pieces.

- If teens enjoy computer games, and you want more in-depth activity, offer a class where they learn to program a computer and make up their own game.

- How could washing dishes possibly be fun? Provide stories on cassette tapes. When a child really gets involved in a taped story, he may actually look forward to listening to the tape while washing dishes. Who knows, he may even enjoy listening to a biographical tape that would benefit his Super Hero's Closet.

- If teens love meat and you want them to eat vegetables, make stuffed meat and vegetable pocket sandwiches.

Attach their pleasure to what you want to promote.

BELONGING

Belonging is a need that teens are especially sensitive to. An overwhelming need to belong can take precedence over all other needs. The chapter on self-esteem explained how to diversify a teen's group of friends, overcoming the corral syndrome, and how to create a positive sense of belonging using positive feedback. How can "belonging" be used to motivate kids?

Mrs. Franck's son had a classic case of the Corral Syndrome. Every day after school, Bill would hang out with the same group of friends at the mall. The sign above his corral read "mallie" (a person who hangs out in a mall). Bill was also doing poorly in school. Mrs. Franck decided to end this behavior by forcing her son to stay home and study. Strains on the family relationship soon became apparent in the form of sullen, non-communicative behavior.

After analyzing her needs, Mrs. Franck decided that the reason she wanted her son, Bill, to study was due to a power need on her part. Bill's future would be affected by his study habits. Mrs. Franck wanted to be able to influence her son's destiny in a positive direction. Her needs had nothing to do with Bill's. He was centered on belonging. This is a common scenario. In these cases, it is better to shift than deny. Find a belonging situation, where the child's needs are satisfied along with the parent's. Studying with a group or getting a friendly peer tutor may satisfy both needs. Involvement in a club with academic leanings may also meet both parent's and child's needs. Mrs. Franck shifted Bill into a study group, arranged for a tutor, and offered choices from a list of clubs with academic value. Occasionally, he visited his mall friends. The home situation improved. So did the grades. You can get what you want when you learn to meet another's needs.

Many parents would like their children to attend college. A need to belong is one way to promote college interest. If you have a friend or older sibling who is attending university, arrange for your child to visit campus for two or three days (visit a new corral). Let the teen feel an attachment to some people. Maybe she talks with a congenial professor, grabs a hamburger in the cafeteria, attends a class of interest, and goes to a basketball or football game surrounded by crowd enthusiasm for the school. If she gets positive feedback, she will feel even better about the experience.

Another step would be to encourage contact with interesting individuals who went to college (you'll notice a little Super Hero's Closet in this). Make it easy for college-oriented teens to be around your child. Invite them over for dinner. Encourage interest groups that feed on academic subjects: computers, SCUBA diving, nature hikes, behind the scenes work at the zoo, reporting for the school paper, foreign travel. Keep her around exciting teachers who take an interest in the child. Remember, the subject may not be the initial spark. It is the "belonging" that encourages many teens to become interested in academic subjects. As she establishes an identity within the group, the subject becomes increasingly important.

Belonging can be used in many contexts to establish motivation. Have you ever noticed a marked change in attitude toward chores when the whole family is involved on a project (this assumes positive feedback is being used)? Why do so many people get involved in walk-a-thons for charity or community service activities? If they had to walk by themselves or sit in an office alone, would there be as much involvement? If you invite your child to a movie, play or museum, does he go into "mope mode?" Then when you suggest making it a party and inviting three or four friends, does it become more palatable? Belonging is an important motivational pedal.

ACHIEVEMENT

Achievement is the fifth pedal. Children with a need to achieve must have certain criteria met. First, they need a moderate challenge. If it is too easy, achievers are bored and produce mediocre work. Shifted to a more demanding environment, achievers often shine. Second, there must be an expectation of success. If it is too hard, achievers back off. When adolescent achievers view something as a remote possibility, they won't waste their time. To encourage achievers, the probability of success must be neither too high nor too low.

Skilled teachers know how to divide a subject into challenging bite-sized chunks. Manageable pieces create an expectation of success. Let's use art as an example. Transferring a picture from mind to paper is a valuable creative skill, yet many teens are adamant that they cannot draw. The approach in this case is to show that a drawing can be broken down into five elements of shape: a dot, circle, straight line, curved line, and angled line. Most children can sketch these lines. Teaching a child to recognize these lines in a drawing would be the first step in teaching sketching. The next step would be to look for these lines in three-dimensional objects. Presented in this manner, children learn to visualize quickly. Success may encourage them to try perspective drawing, shading, and other artistic endeavors.

The art of motivating achievers consists of dividing subjects into manageable pieces.

Success builds on success. Do you remember spelling bees? If you were a poor speller, it was an opportunity to embarrass yourself. Modern teachers, recognizing the negative aspects of the "bee," have added a twist. At the beginning of each week, teachers use a test to find which words a child can spell from a pre-arranged list. During spelling bees, students have the choice of spelling a difficult, moderate, or easy word. Their team receives one, two, or three points depending on the difficulty of the word for that child. In this way, both good and poor spellers have the potential of contributing points to their team and spelling improves greatly. This modified spelling bee allows the child to aim for a reasonable level of challenge and success.

There are several methods of horse training. One is to break a horse in a wild, bucking bronco ride. The drawback of bronco busting is that such horses are often unreliable and inconsistent. A second method is blanket training. Blanket training involves small steps. First, you secure the horse in a pen and rub it down with a riding blanket. Initially, the horse is skittish. When it calms down, the next step is to slip the blanket on and off the horse's back many times. Next, the saddle is repeatedly slipped on and off. Eventually, the horse is ready for the rider to add weight to the stirrup. The process continues until you have a rideable horse. Blanket training instills confidence. Success at each step builds toward the next success. Why go to all this trouble? Blanket trained horses display more confidence, consistency, and reliability than broken horses.

Adolescent achievers prefer activities that produce immediate results. They want to see, hear, or feel the outcome right away. Building a model, sewing a skirt, playing a guitar, or sketching a poodle are examples of activities that provide immediate feedback. Properly assembled, a model's parts fit together; good sewing creates a neat hem; correctly strummed, a C chord sounds right; and the drawing either looks like a poodle or it doesn't. Achievers don't like to wait for an outside source to judge their progress. They are their own judges.

Steve Wozniak, the genius who developed the Apple computer, had this to say about achievement as a child: "I would always think of a project in my mind first, then draw it on paper. I'd pull out a ruler and some colored pencils and draw very accurately. I'd feel proud about it and want it to look neat. I wasn't going to show it to anyone, or get a higher grade in school, or get a salary. There was an internal reward. I knew it was mine and that I had done a good job."

Educators who work with achievement-oriented teens need to realize that these children derive their satisfaction from concrete activities that give immediate performance feedback, Wozniak's "internal reward." School does not always provide rapid feedback. Studying for a history exam, learning the usage of nouns and adjectives, and memorizing the periodic chart in chemistry all lack immediate concrete performance incentives. Teachers have to find ways to give achievers their "internal rewards." Computer-programmed learning is one answer. Computers can supply the immediate feedback that motivates achievers. A computer can pose a question and then give immediate feedback on the child's response. A side benefit of computer-aided study is that children can travel at their own pace so they aren't bored, an important consideration with achievers.

To foster an achiever:

1. Maintain challenge to maintain interest. Too easy and achievers slack off.

2. Guarantee a reasonable probability of success by dividing a challenge into bite-sized chunks. Think in terms of blanket training.

3. Achievers prefer activities that provide immediate concrete results. They like to judge their own progress.

POWER

Power is the final set of pedals. The chapter on self-esteem mentioned the importance of giving teens the feeling that they have control over their destiny. Power is often the "need" that impels people to get an education, pursue money, develop skills, seek social contacts, exercise, and accept leadership positions — all because they want a feeling of control over their future. In the self-esteem framework, chores were used as an example of how to build power. Here are other examples of ways to satisfy the power incentive and, at the same time, meet your needs:

- In small midwestern schools where a teacher teaches multiple grades, older students get the responsibility of tutoring younger students. This technique produces surprising results. Students from these small schools often do better on college entrance exams than students from major metropolitan high schools. The responsibility of tutoring encourages older students to better understand subjects so they can do a better job of teaching. The younger students, in turn, get personal attention. It follows the old adage, the best way to learn a subject is to teach it.

- In a step-by-step program (e.g., blanket training), some parents prepare their children for monetary responsibility. They build up to allowances of $100 or more per month. Did I hear an in-rush of breath? A $100 allowance? Yes. But this allowance covers everything from clothing to books, shoes to entertainment. Parents who have prepared their children for these mega-allowances say they spend less money per year than they used to because they don't get nickeled and dimed to death. The child has obvious control of her destiny.

- To promote responsibility, one family made the children's allowances dependent on operating a small garden in the backyard. The children's allowances were related to the produce they put on the table. The children then had control over their cash flow.

- Getting a part-time job can meet the power need of many children and satisfy the achievement needs of many parents. Job possibilities include babysitting, pet-sitting, paper routes, tutoring, gardening, go-fer at a parent's work place, and junior counselor at a summer camp. If your child wants to start her own business, there are two books that can provide her with ideas: *Teenage Entrepreneur's Guide* by Sarah Riehm (Surrey Books, (312) 751-7330, $10.95) and *Fast Cash for Kids* by Bonnie and Noel Drew (Homeland Publications, 1808 Capri Lane, Seabrook, TX 77586, $12.50). To help young people set up a profitable business, *Busines$ Kids* sells a starter kit for $49.95 (1-800-852-4544). One feature of the kit is a subscription to a motivational newsletter. A recent newsletter contained the story of ten-year old Brandon Bozek who used the principles in the kit to start a flower delivery service, *Bloomin' Express*. He makes a profit of $75 a month.

- Maybe you want to avoid unpleasant confrontations with your child over rules. In the next chapter, we discuss how to involve teens in their own discipline. Giving children power in designing rules and consequences often satisfies a power need and results in better adherence to the accepted rules.

USING THE MOTIVATIONAL PEDALS

Let's see how the motivational pedals would be used in a real-life scenario. Ms. Kraft wants her daughter, Delia, to be more social, to have a greater sense of belonging. Every day, it's the same thing: Delia comes home after school and plops in front of the TV or plugs into a Walkman. Sorting through the motivational pedals, Ms. Kraft comes up with avoidance as the motive for Delia's behavior. Delia has low self-esteem. Subconsciously, she realizes that teens, like sharks, sense weakness. Delia fears exposing the soft underbelly of her self-worth. She avoids criticism from other teens by retreating to the television and Walkman. Ms. Kraft has to consider her daughter's avoidance need when trying to establish social interaction.

The first small step was encouraged through babysitting. Babysitters find that age alone confers status in a little kid's eyes. Without risk, Delia was encouraged to start belonging. As time went on, there were opportunities to babysit older kids (notice the blanket training). Later still, Delia started work in a convalescent hospital. What do the elderly love? "Delia, you said you'd sit with me today." "Delia, come in and play some cards." Delia's company was much appreciated. Eventually, Delia's self-esteem was healthy enough that she ventured to meet with peers. This stage was reached by providing Delia what she needed, avoidance of risk to her self-esteem. By being patient (outlasting), Ms. Kraft got what she wanted, and her child expanded her social contacts and had a greater sense of belonging.

Think in terms of the six needs each time you want to effect a change in behavior. Link your needs and your teen's needs together so you both get what you want.

WILEY FOX'S LESSON ON MOTIVATION

Wiley Fox sought to be chief of the animal tribe. Before he could do so, he would have to seek counsel from the most powerful animal in the forest, a grizzly. The wise Medicine Owl explained to Wiley that the meeting with Grizzly was very important. If Wiley Fox was worthy, Grizzly would grant a single wish — a wish that would reveal the secret of being a great chief.

With that, Wiley Fox entered the forest. It was not long before a mighty grizzly appeared, a fearsome beast the size of a mountain. Wiley stood his ground, which spoke well of his courage. As the huge bear approached, Wiley made gestures of peace and explained what he wanted. But Grizzly gnashed teeth and reared up with a roar.

The meeting did not appear to be going well.

Wiley Fox pawed rapidly through the sack slung over his back and came up with some food that he tossed to the grizzly. But Grizzly only growled like a great thunderstorm and the ground shook with each step.

Wiley grabbed a spear and held it in his shaking paws, but still Grizzly came forward. Just as Grizzly was ready to fall on him, Wiley spoke, "Oh Great Grizzly, please spare my life."

Suddenly, Wiley heard a soft mewing sound. Cautiously he looked over his shoulder.

Two frightened cubs stared at their mother. Quickly, Wiley scrambled aside and Mother Grizzly lumbered past to her cubs.

Later when he was back with the tribe, Medicine Owl asked Wiley if he had learned the secret of being a good leader.

Wiley nodded. "Grizzly taught me an important lesson. When I first met Grizzly, I told her what I WANTED. And she ignored me. Then I DECIDED what it was she wanted, and I offered food that she crushed under her feet. Finally, I THREATENED her with my spear like a tiny raindrop against a burning tree. As her shadow covered the sun, I begged her to spare my life. It was then I heard her cubs cry and I knew what she NEEDED. As I hurried out of the way, she in turn granted my wish and spared my life. And it was then that I learned the secret of being a great leader."

> To the degree you meet others' needs, they will meet yours.

MOTIVATIONAL NEEDS SUMMARY

The six motivational needs:

SURVIVAL

AVOIDANCE

PLEASURE

BELONGING

ACHIEVEMENT

POWER

6

THE DISCIPLINE BRAKES

Updating An Old Standby — Discipline In The 90's

Discipline should be used like irreplaceable brakepads, sparingly and wisely. A parent in one of my workshops was exasperated by her teen's rebellious attitude. It turned out that, over the years, Mom had made a list for her teen's conduct. This list contained 122 rules, everything from where to put shoes in the closet to how the table should be set. Many concerns mentioned were trivial in the larger scheme of things, and the son was constantly being penalized for errors. Rapport in the relationship was going downhill, as was the son's positive sense of belonging. Many changes the mother wanted could have been accomplished with *feedback to change behavior* (see Chapter 3).

Discipline brakes are reserved for the steep hills. Discipline is necessary when other methods don't work and unwanted behavior can dramatically affect the quality of life. Causes for applying discipline generally fall into six categories:

1. CURFEW: Your son cruises in two hours past curfew.

2. CHORES: Your son leaves the dirty dishes stacked in the sink — again.

3. SCHOOLWORK: Your daughter has a stronger preference for TV than homework. Her report card has three D's.

4. BOY-GIRL RELATIONSHIPS: Your fourteen-year old daughter's overt displays of affection with her boyfriend make you uncomfortable.

5. BANNED SUBSTANCES: While driving home, you pass your daughter. A cigarette dangles from her lips.

6. DISRESPECT: You ask your son to pick up his jacket, books, and gym clothes that are strewn over the living room. He replies by calling you a jerk.

Cyclists know that brakes, used improperly, can be dangerous. Racing down a hill and suddenly applying the front brakes will throw a rider over the handlebars. Effective braking follows a pattern — rear brakes are applied first, then the front ones. Effective discipline also follows a pattern:

1. Arrange for a meeting to set up a behavior contract.
2. Involve the teen in designing the contract.
3. Pre-arrange consequences that are logically related to the misdeed.
4. Consistently enforce the agreement.

ARRANGE A MEETING TO SET UP A BEHAVIOR CONTRACT

If there are indications that a teen is teetering on the brink of a steep hill, discipline starts by scheduling a meeting. Arrange a calm time to sit and talk with your child (avoid heat-of-the-moment confrontations). The purpose of this meeting is to prepare a behavior contract. A behavior contract defines acceptable behavior and spells out consequences for misbehavior.

A good way to maintain a relationship is to set up pre-arranged meetings — even when there aren't problems. Routine meetings establish an expectation that family members are all involved in the planning and carrying out of family life. Such meetings can be used to plan trips, give reinforcing feedback, air grievances, discuss solutions to problems, and handle discipline. Family meetings are a good habit.

INVOLVE THE CHILD

Involve your child in setting up a behavior contract. Remember that power, a sense of control over one's destiny, is an element of self-esteem. By including teens in the disciplinary process, you share power. You are also applying the original meaning of the word 'discipline,' *to teach.* Teens learn by experience. Setting up a contract shows that discipline is not an arbitrary process to satisfy a vindictive parent. This helps children develop inner discipline.

Start out by explaining your concern in a short, tight sentence. For example, "I would like the dishes washed and put away by 6:00," or "Words like 'jerk' make me feel bad and I want to avoid that type of feeling." Using an I-message format helps maintain good communication.

Now that you have stated your concerns in a positive manner, ask for the teen's viewpoint. Before the child starts, take some tape and put it across your lips. Make it clear that you are going to listen to his concerns. A dialog might go something like this:

"Kevin, I start imagining things and worry when my son isn't home by 9:00. I'd like a 9:00 curfew. Is that a reasonable time to be in?" (This is the point to tape your lips shut until your child has finished speaking.)

"Geez, Dad, the movies don't get out until 10:00. Then, we usually go for a hamburger. All the guys will think I'm a wimpoid."

If the child has trouble presenting his point of view, you might use *reflective listening* (see Chapter 2) to clarify his perspective.

When both sides are stated, tell your teen that you are open to brainstorming alternate possibilities. How can your needs as well as your teen's be met? Use a pad of paper to write down ideas. Writing down a teen's suggestions signifies a level of respect. You contribute as well, writing down your suggestions.

Make it clear that suggestions will not be judged until the end of the brainstorming session. Making judgments while brainstorming turns a downpour into a drizzle.

When you run out of ideas, go back through the list and discuss what is acceptable to you and what the teen feels good about. A brainstorming session over curfew might go something like this:

"Kevin, I start imagining things and worry when my son isn't home by 9:00. I'd like a 9:00 curfew. I understand from what you say that it might cramp your style when you're out with friends. Like the movies don't even get out until 10:00. [Notice the use of reflective listening in the reply.] Let's do some brainstorming and see if we can come up with something that will meet my needs and yours as well."

"Well, you could just not worry."

"Let me write that one down. What else?"

"I could tell you where we will be."

"OK. How about one of mine? You call home at 9:00 if you're going to be late."

"But Dad, movies go until 10:00 and I'd have to get up and go to the lobby and ..."

"Remember, no judges permitted in the brainstorming sessions."

"Oh yeah. What about you buy me a portable telephone?"

"Kevin, let's keep it reasonable."

"Remember, Dad. No judges permitted in brainstorming sessions."

"OK, point taken. How about your mother or I pick you up and drop you off anyplace you will be after 9:00?"

"What if I leave a note about when the movie starts and ends?"

"Any more ideas?"

"Nope."

"Let's see what we've got."

After going through the list, the parent and teen compromise. The teen will post a list on the refrigerator of where he will be. On the list, he will write down the ending time of any movie or event. If the teen is doing anything after the event, he will call and okay it with the parent. The maximum curfew allowable with the new rules is pushed up to 11:00. Both the parent's concern of knowing where his child is at night and the teen's desire for a more flexible curfew are met. This rule is written out as part of the behavior contract.

Involvement of teens in setting up rules alters their perspective on discipline, resulting in less alienation and resentment. Older children recognize fairness. They can tell when their rights are being respected. Their involvement is also required in the next phase of the behavior contract, setting up consequences.

CONSEQUENCES LOGICALLY RELATED TO THE MISDEED

Just as you wrote down your rules, write down your consequences. Involving teens in choosing consequences will help them understand the next half of discipline.

There are three types of consequences: punitive, restrictive, and instructive. *Punitive consequences* are primal forms of behavior control such as a whack on the behind. Without getting into the ethics of punitive control, suffice it to say that it damages rapport, especially with teens. Lowered rapport means less effective motivation.

Restrictive consequences result in a loss of freedom: early to bed, removal of entertainment, a cut in allowance, restriction to room, prevented from seeing friends.

Instructive consequences enforce new behavior: compulsory study hours, required community service, increased responsibility.

In choosing a consequence, get help from the child. Try to find a penalty that is logically related to the misdeed. This elevates discipline to the level of instruction. Consider the following logical consequences:

- Curfew: Kevin comes in an hour past curfew. He knows this means he will lose his privilege of going out for two weekends.

- Chores: Michael has again forgotten to put the garbage can on the curb for the garbage truck. He is reminded about his agreement. Now he must separate the trash and crush the cans and boxes so they take up less room. Then he bags the trash and stores it next to his bike in the garage. (Remember the importance of upgrading chore levels and be willing to share the responsibility for mundane tasks.)

- Schoolwork: Amy comes home with a D in math. Amy's mother grounds her by pulling the plug. She pulls the plug on the TV, stereo, radio, and phone. Amy is barred from spending time with the entertainment thieves that steal her study time. Pulling the plug is a form of high tech, restrictive grounding.

  Next, Amy is required to attend TEAM. TEAM is an after-school period at Amy's school in which students ask teachers questions about classwork. Attending TEAM represents instructive grounding.

  Asked how she felt about being grounded, Amy replied that it seemed to be helping her, and she probably would do the same thing if she had children with a similar problem. Children see the logic when grounding is applied that has a relation to their misdeed.

- Boy-girl relationships: Mr. Regis is concerned about his fourteen-year old daughter and her boyfriend. Innocent hand-holding has escalated to lots of hugging, lap-sitting, and groping. Mr. Regis has tried I-messages to no avail. Finally, he confronts his daughter with a two-part logical consequence. Overt physical displays of affection will result in calling the boy's parents and arranging a meeting to discuss the behavior. In addition, his daughter will donate a prescribed amount of time at a day care center. The father feels that this will open his daughter's eyes to what it means to care for a child.

The Evolution of Discipline

- Banned substances: Ms. Maples smells alcohol on her daughter's breath. She confronts her daughter and simply says, "Remember our agreement? The Alcoholics Anonymous meeting is Thursday night."

- Disrespect: An occasional verbal outburst might be handled with an I-message response. A recurring problem requires a different tack. This is an important time to remember, My Purpose Is Not To Win, It Is To Outlast. Some logical consequences might be to arrange time to sit and discuss your differences calmly, or provide reading material that encourages your teen to look at things from another person's perspective. (Joyce Vedral's books, *My Parents Are Driving Me Crazy* and *My Teenager is Driving Me Crazy*, offer good sources for exploring the parental and teen perspectives.) Another possibility is to arrange to have a counselor act as an intermediary in a dispute.

  In severe cases, consider a *Toughlove* program. (For information on *Toughlove* programs in your area, write: P.O. Box 10069, Doylestown, PA, 18901. Phone: 1-800-333-1069. You can also order a *Toughlove* videotape from Fries Home Video, 6922 Hollywood Blvd., Hollywood, CA 90028. This video is a dramatization of how *Toughlove* works. The video is not a substitute for attending meetings.)

Penalties unrelated to the misdeed are less effective. Scott was supposed to babysit his younger brother. Instead, he sent his brother to a neighbor's house to play while Scott went off with friends. When Scott's parents found out, part of his punishment was to stay in his room for five hours. "Staying in my room for five hours," said Scott, "was punishment that didn't prove anything."

When asked how he would have handled the problem, Scott replied, "Maybe I should have been made to babysit for two weekends in a row to learn responsibility. They could explain what would happen if I made the mistake again." Scott's suggested penalty is logical and a form of instructive grounding.

When your eleven-year old has just cruised in two hours past curfew, it is difficult to control emotions and select rational consequences. This is the reason for having a behavior contract. If your child misses curfew, there is no need to rant and rave, consequences are pre-arranged. A behavior contract spells out acceptable behavior and the consequences of not adhering to this behavior. Rational consequences are not easy to come up with. Sometimes you may not discover a logical repercussion. By involving teens in this difficult part of discipline, you broaden their perspective and it makes the next phase of discipline less stressful.

ENFORCEMENT

Rules work only when consistently enforced. To illustrate this point during workshops, I ask a volunteer to do the following:

"Please stand on this chair. Lock your hands behind your back. Now lean forward and touch your nose to the ground — without taking your feet off the chair."

They go through a few contortions, then announce, "It can't be done."

"Sure it can. If you keep leaning forward, and keep your feet on the stool, I guarantee that your nose will touch the ground."

We avoid falling on our faces because we know that Mother Nature consistently enforces her rules — especially the rule on gravity. Parents should follow Mother Nature's example when it applies to enforcing consequences.

Inconsistency undermines a parent's credibility. As one teenager said, "Some kids say they are grounded, then their parents give in ... kids think they've gotten away with it." If consequences are applied as consistently as gravity, children associate inappropriate behavior with a penalty and are more likely to change their behavior.

Behavior contracts are set up because it is easier to enforce penalties that have been pre-arranged. Punishments created during the heat of confrontation may not be balanced to the magnitude of the misdeed. For instance:

> "How dare you call me a jerk. Go to your room. You're grounded for the rest of the month and you're not to see any of your friends."

After cooling off, the parent decides the penalty is illogical and excessive. Now Mom is caught in a Catch-22 situation. If she backs down, she loses credibility. If she doesn't back down, she's forced to carry out an unfair ultimatum that damages the parent/child relationship. Pre-arranging consequences helps parents avoid this trap.

It is easier to enforce discipline that you believe will benefit your child. It is even easier if your child has been involved in the decision process. This is the reason for a behavior contract. It pre-arranges rational penalties. By involving a child in fashioning the contract, you show respect for his rights. It demonstrates to the child that you view discipline as a learning process.

DISCIPLINE SUMMARY

Discipline is more effective when it is thought out in advance.

1. Arrange for a meeting to set up a behavior contract.
2. Involve the teen in designing the contract.
3. Pre-arrange consequences that are logically related to the misdeed.
4. Consistently enforce the agreement.

Parent Power In Your Wildest Dreams

7

THE ATTITUDE GEARS

Building A Good Attitude

Some gears are easier to pedal in than others. When assembling a motivational bicycle, it is important to install positive attitude gears. Positive attitude gears enable children to take on terrain where most would fail. A positive attitude is a characteristic of self-motivated children.

Simply telling a teenager to change his attitude is not going to have much effect. From a teenager's perspective, "attitude" is an abstract term with little meaning. Teenagers believe that sticks and stones may break their bones, but "attitude" will never hurt them.

To be significant to a teenager, "attitude" must be transformed into something with weight and texture. There are two ways to accomplish this transformation. The first is to tell stories about attitude. The second method is to have attitude workouts.

A compelling story, whether factual or metaphorical, can have tremendous impact on a child's attitude. Research has shown that folktales and myths often parallel attitudes held by entire cultures, from preliterate tribes to modern corporate empires. Stories can shape attitude. But to have the greatest influence, words must also be attached to experience — in this case, *attitude workouts.*

Attitude workouts are practical exercises in attitude control. Many teens believe they have no control over their attitude. Their attitude is a balloon at the mercy of the wind. Attitude workouts offer an opportunity to show teens that they can pilot their attitude. Parents who prepare their children with attitude workouts will find that life is much easier. Trying to change an attitude during the heat of confrontation is counter-productive. Conduct attitude workouts at calm times.

Let's look at some concrete examples of attitude stories and workouts:

FOUR ATTITUDE STORIES

The first chapter of this book discussed the importance of converting abstract ideas into something teens can understand. Telling stories to a teen at the appropriate time can have a profound impact on attitude. Stories give concrete definition to an otherwise hazy idea. Each of the following stories points out an important feature related to having a positive attitude. You may also know stories you want to share with teens.

The Importance Of Attitude: The Prison Camp

My dad was captured at the beginning of World War II. Confined in a Japanese prison camp, he suffered beatings, forced marches, malnutrition, and disease. Every morning he checked one vital possession — his attitude. Each day he swore he would survive. My father was intensely aware of the importance of his attitude.

Occasionally, new prisoners were brought to camp. They had not suffered prolonged deprivation. Many of them were healthy, and yet they would go off in a corner, curl up — and die. Overwhelmed by conditions, they chose an attitude that literally kills. Psychologists call it *prison camp death syndrome*. After four and a half years, my father was freed. He had dropped from 180 to 90 pounds. His attitude saved his life.

The first step toward changing an attitude is instilling a realization of how important attitude is. In a dramatic fashion, the prison camp story points out that attitude can literally make the difference between life and death. The story also illustrates that attitude is a choice. My father was exposed to the same outside conditions as the new prisoners, probably worse considering his long captivity, yet inside he maintained a positive survival attitude. Outside circumstances seem to control attitude but, in reality, each individual decides which attitude he or she will accept.

> The world can shape your attitude
> or your attitude can shape the world.

Controlling Attitude: Doves And Vultures

Metaphorical stories make it easier for teens to grasp an abstract message. The following story was devised to help a thirteen-year old in the aftermath of a traumatic experience. She described her attitude in the following way: "I have these unhappy thoughts that just come in and I can't keep them out." This story helped her get control over the negativity that was making her life miserable:

Your mind is a tree. Your thoughts are like two birds — doves and vultures. Doves are positive, uplifting thoughts. If they perch in your mind, you'll hear, "You got a handle on it. This is a great day — try missing one. Get down to work and you'll get on top of it. Extraordinary people are ordinary people with extraordinary amounts of determination."

The other bird is the vulture. These are negative thoughts. If you feel their scrabbly claws gripping your branches, you'll hear, "Why's a braindead mutant like you trying to do math? Don't let no lightbulbs go off in that vacuum center between your ears, you're couch potato material. Whoa Kemo Sabe, I think those girls/boys are talking about you. Did I hear them say turbojerk?"

When buzzards swoop down, doves scatter. It's the old adage, birds of a feather flock together.

It's possible to "see" attitude. You can spot a buzzard roost. Do you know anyone who has a tree filled with buzzards? You can also "see" attitude in people who have a tree filled with doves. Do you know anyone who has a "dove" attitude?

Vultures can be kept from roosting by carrying a vulture shotgun. When a negative thought comes flapping in, imagine a positive action that would improve the situation. This positive action is the ammunition needed to clear buzzards out of the air. Teens should always carry positive ammunition. If a teen sees a vulture headed in for a landing like, "I'm the stupidest person on earth," fire away with, "I'm going to sit down now and study for one hour." If the vulture says, "No one is ever going to ask me out," blast it out of the air with, "I'll ask Tony if he would like to study history at the library." Or, if a vulture whispers, "My parents don't understand me," load up with, "I need to talk with my parents tonight."

Vultures drag people down and leave nothing but bones. Doves lift people up. The easiest and hardest lesson for teens to learn is that choosing doves over vultures is just that — a choice. The young girl mentioned earlier learned to visualize her "bad thoughts" as vultures. This made it easier for her to take aim and shoot them out of the air so that doves had a place to land.

Turning An Attitude Around: The Blind Men

In life, there are "things" you have to do. Teens often think their list is exceptionally long: go to school, be home by curfew, pick up your stuff, mow the lawn ... Sometimes they develop a negative attitude about things required of them. This story will help teens seek the positive side of situations.

There was a village in India where everyone was blind except the headman. It was the headman's job to teach the sightless about the world. One day he brought a strange thing to the village square. He asked Akmed to explore the object and say what he thought. Akmed felt with his hands and pronounced, "It is a great wall."

Next was Raoul. His hands quickly searched and he announced, "It is four great oak trees, the trunks solidly rooted to the ground."

Crotchety Shaki said, "You are both fools. It is nothing more than a great flapping bird's wing."

In the meantime, Moski argued with Falal. One of them swore it was no thicker than a rope. The other said it was like a massive python.

The blind men were in a great debate until the headman silenced their squabble, "It is an elephant: the wall, his body; the four oak trees, his legs; the flapping bird wing, an ear; the rope, its tail; and the python, its trunk."

We are all blind. We see only a portion of what shapes our attitude. Teens who wish to lead themselves need to see the whole elephant. They can do this by listing five positive things

Look at your elephant

about any situation that is giving them a negative attitude. As an example, look at what one teenager wrote about a common attitude problem, "School is a drag."

Upon closer inspection of his elephant, he discovered five benefits of going to school:

1. School provides me with a social life — dances, ski trips, clubs. A bunch of friends in one place.
2. If I do well in school, I've got a better chance of getting an interesting job.
3. School's the reason I can make change, read street signs, and fill out a job application.
4. I love organized sports and school makes that possible.
5. I've learned how to concentrate, which will help me learn things I'm interested in later.

Whenever there is something you've gotta' do and negativity blinds your attitude, LOOK AT YOUR ELEPHANT. Find five positive things about the situation, and make the best of it.

Dealing With A Universal Attitude Problem: The Monster T'NACI*

This attitude story is one of my favorites. It never fails to have an impact on the children who hear it.

When Roland was a child, he dreamed of running with the wind and climbing mountains to touch the sun and the moon. Then one day he found a tiny creature. A T'NACI. Roland's parents had not warned him about T'NACI. Unknowingly, he picked up the tiny beast. It

---

* Pronounced Te-nac-kee

seemed harmless. In time, Roland became fond of T'NACI and carried it in his shirt pocket wherever he went.

T'NACI was content to munch quietly on scraps — and grow. Soon it was too big for a shirt pocket. So it went into a bookpack. It rode everywhere on Roland's back. When T'NACI outgrew the pack, Roland built a cart and attached a harness so he could pull T'NACI with him. The scraps had turned into chunks to appease the growing T'NACI's appetite.

Roland's friends, who loved to run, saw that Roland could not keep up. The cart with the growing T'NACI slowed him down. Roland needed friends who carried their personal T'NACIs. These were the only people he could keep up with. Roland felt miserable, but he was attached to T'NACI. When asked to give the creature up, he shook his head sadly. He had spent so much time with the creature, he could not imagine parting with it.

As the years progressed, T'NACI grew into a sizable monster. No longer did Roland dream of running with the wind and he did not think of touching the sun and the moon. Dragging a cart with a large monster makes running very difficult. And the sun and moon can only be reached by climbing mountains. Who wants to pull a heavy monster up a mountain?

One day when Roland was very old, he dragged his cart by a lake and saw the reflection of his monster in the water. Then he realized what T'NACI really was. If you look at the picture of T'NACI (page 157) in a mirror, you will see what Roland saw.

T'NACI is like a cockroach or rat. Garbage attracts the monster. To survive, it must feed on the garbage of fear. There are four fears it thrives on:

Hold this picture up to a mirror and you will see what Roland saw
reflected in the water.

1. *Fear of failure.* Roland was going to try out for the basketball team, then he thought, "I can't shoot baskets very well. Everyone else is probably better, so why waste the time?"

2. *Fear of rejection.* Roland was going to ask Alicia to the dance. Then he thought, "What if she turns me down? I can't deal with that." So he didn't ask.

3. *Fear of change.* Roland was moving. He thought, "I can't ever find any friends as good as the ones I had in the old neighborhood." He was very miserable.

4. *Fear of success.* Things were going well for Roland, then a thought came into his mind, "I can't expect this good luck to continue. I just know something bad is going to happen."

Each fear is like throwing a chunk of meat to T'NACI. Feeding T'NACI makes him fat. The heavier he gets, the harder he is to pull.

Some argue that fear is good. They say that walking through a crime-ridden section of the city late at night is a good fear. But there is an important distinction between, "I CAN'T walk through the city late at night," and "I choose not to walk through the city late at night because the risks outweigh any benefits." Fear takes the choice out of a teen's hands and puts it in T'NACI's claws.

T'NACI gnaws at the backbone of motivation. Every time a child mutters "I CAN'T," he offers a tidbit of fear for T'NACI to chew on. "I CAN'T" blocks the mind from facing challenges. It is an addictive phrase that focuses the speaker on the insolubility of problems.

Without "I CAN'T," children must come to grips with why they aren't doing something. To safeguard a teen from acquiring a T'NACI monster, eradicate "I CAN'T" from a child's vocabulary. Start by telling children the T'NACI story. Then encourage children to substitute the word "T'NACI" for the phrase "I CAN'T."

T'NACI ask Ellen out for a date.

T'NACI do math.

T'NACI clean up my room.

If it feels unnatural, good, that's its purpose. When children become aware of the monster, they are less likely to feed him. If teens erase "I CAN'T" from their vocabulary, they leap up a notch on the success ladder. Think in terms of what I can do, not what T'NACI do.

ATTITUDE WORKOUTS

When I started my career as a university water polo coach, I inherited a team with a reputation for uncontrollable tempers. Their attitude was "If an opponent fouls you, sock him in the head." They considered themselves tough. They were so tough, they were consistently ejected from the game. Their attitude made them a losing team.

First I tried talking. It didn't help. Then I tried discipline, with marginal success.

Finally, I decided to have an attitude workout. During a scrimmage, I informed players that one individual on each team was going to be a sitting duck. It was open season on that player. A sitting duck was unprotected by the referee. Within reason, you could grab him, hold him underwater, swim over him, and the ref would be blind. If the designated player talked back to the ref, he would be ejected from the game. Only members on the opposing team knew which player was the sitting duck. In this way, opposing players didn't know if they were the marked player or simply being fouled and it wasn't caught.

After scrimmages, I focused on reinforcing feedback. Players were praised for "toughness" if they could handle the fouling and stay cool. In a short time, players were proud of their ability to keep swimming down the pool with an opposing player hanging on their suit or grabbing their ankles. In the locker room, they'd talk about a sitting duck who had managed to score a goal while being stuffed underwater. Needless to say, performance in real games improved.

Attitude improves more rapidly when exercises are provided during which awareness and control can be practiced. The following exercises help teens become aware of their attitude and develop an attitude that leads to winning performance.

To make a teen aware of his attitude, try this. Have him carry a felt tip pen in his pocket. Every time he has a positive dove thought, he puts a mark on his left hand. Each time a negative buzzard thought perches in his tree, the teen puts a mark on his right hand. See how much control he has over his buzzards and doves by comparing the marks at the end of the day.

A variation on the felt tip pen is to have a teen carry a pocket full of dimes. Every time a buzzard swoops in, the teen takes a dime and tosses it on the ground. If she catches herself and shoots the buzzard out of the air by coming up with a positive thought, she holds on to the dime. See how many dimes she has at the end of a day or week.

To teach teens how to maintain a positive attitude in a confrontational setting, play a game called *attitude challenge*. To play, divide the group in half. You can play with as few as two people. One group becomes the challengers, they get to act. Challengers are provided with a barbed topic, such as "Dinner is gross." Each challenger chooses a partner from the other group. The partner's goal is to maintain a positive attitude throughout the exchange. To do this, the confronted partner practices communication skills learned earlier, such as reflective listening, I-messages, and open-ended questions (see Chapter 2). When the timer says go, the action begins. The exchange lasts one minute. When the timer says stop, partners switch roles and start a new topic such as, "Why do you have to dress like such a wierdo?" Going back and forth like this lets teens practice keeping their attitude on an even keel. You will notice that it also helps a teen see the world from an alternate perspective.

Deer Crossing's *Leaders In Training* (LIT) program offers older teens an opportunity to work on their attitude through a variety of exercises. One exercise is the LIT Quest. During LIT Quests, students hike to a high altitude in the Sierra. Each LIT's equipment consists of personal clothing, several fishhooks, a match, a knife, water purification tablets, a bottle, and one granola bar. For three days, under survival conditions, the LIT's goal is to attract doves and keep buzzards away. Supervising instructors explain that complaining terminates a Quest. Students are to seek solutions rather than dwell on problems.

As challenging as LIT Quests are, students have consistently displayed positive energy. One of our LITs exemplified this spirit when she saved her granola bar till the last day of a Quest and shared it with her companions. Teens who control their attitude can shape it to their benefit.

Pedaling through life with license plates that read BD A2TUD (Bad Attitude) may give teens the impression that they are in control of their lives. More likely, circumstances control them. Attitude awareness and workouts can help teens change their plates to GD A2TUD.

CONCLUSION

The Motivational Bicycle Assembled

In the first chapter, motivation was likened to a bicycle composed of seven parts: Perspective Mirror, Communication Horn, Self-esteem Frame, Goal Setting Handlebars and Wheels, Need Pedals, Discipline Brakes, and Attitude Gears. Anyone who has assembled a bicycle knows that if you leave out parts, it either wobbles or grinds to a halt.

In my seminars, there is usually someone who wants to throw away a part because it doesn't produce the desired result 100% of the time. They fail to see the whole machine. For instance, using feedback to change behavior may not work as smoothly as the examples presented in Chapter 3. Maybe feedback produces the desired result only 80% of the time. This doesn't negate the significance of feedback. It simply means you shift to another technique that is more appropriate to the situation. Maybe the teen needs help with goal steering, or possibly discipline is required, or maybe you need to talk in more concrete terms, or do away with words altogether and find an experience that motivates. Successful motivators are flexible motivators. They rely on multiple techniques.

The beauty of the strategy in this book is that the techniques are complementary. They mesh smoothly, like bicycle gears, to deliver maximum power. If a single method does not produce the desired result, you simply add another technique. The seven techniques covered in this book are designed to be piggybacked, one on top of another, to increase your motivational impact.

Enhancing persuasive power by piggybacking is an important concept. Let me illustrate piggybacking with two examples:

THE PUT-DOWN ARTIST

Fifteen-year old Bob, one of our new campers, relished "cutting" people down. He wielded criticism like a razor. He could flay a sensitive teen with his Cuisinart sarcasm. Even adults were vulnerable to his verbal jabs. Bob's stature was built on chopping other people down.

An adult's first impulse, when dealing with a put-down artist, is to parry and stab back, to win. But losing would not solve Bob's problem. Bob's negative behavior was due to a lack of self-confidence. From Bob's *perspective,* cutting other people down made him superior. It was also destroying his chance for making friends. While Bob was attending camp, we hoped to outlast his put-downs and motivate him toward more constructive behavior.

To turn Bob's behavior around, instructors started using *reinforcing feedback* to focus on his good traits. When Bob helped someone, such as giving assistance in carrying a windsurf board or offering verbal support for someone else's effort, he received specific praise.

To shift Bob from a fault-finder to a solution-finder, instructors used *feedback to change behavior.* When Bob started to offer a critical comment, we asked him to state what he wanted to see as the outcome: "Bob, we aren't interested in what a person has done wrong. We want to know what they have to do to make it right." If Bob was working with someone in a canoe, rather than call the person "braindead" because of a mistake, we told Bob to give a specific command, such as, "Pull stroke on your right."

Both forms of feedback were used to build Bob's positive *sense of belonging* which would ultimately contribute to his self-esteem. With more personal self-esteem, he would have less incentive to criticize.

Next we analyzed Bob's needs. It was obvious that he derived pleasure from being sarcastic in front of a group. How could we combine that *pleasure need* with a healthy outlet? Instructors decided to encourage Bob to enter an improvisational comedy class. In such a class, he could perform. The improv instructor concentrated on developing humor in place of caustic remarks. When his wit was guided away from hurtful comments, he displayed a genuine comedic wit and an ability to think on his feet. The comedy instructor piggybacked this ability into *magic key words*:

> "Bob, that pause just before the punch line created the tension you needed for a laugh. That shows *comedic sense*."
>
> "Those rapid replies are an example of *thinking on your feet*."

Magic key words helped focus Bob on his unique positive qualities.

Improvisational comedy provided Bob with a specific *experience* where he could feel self-confident and work on supporting other cast members. In this positive environment, Bob became aware that his stage performance was a team effort. Only by supporting other members of the cast could he establish the trust and relaxation necessary for good improv comedy. It was to Bob's benefit to encourage his friends, rather than cut them down.

Because Bob's need for performing was being satisfied, he showed up regularly for classes. He was self-motivated to attend.

To counteract Bob's negativity, an *attitude story* was shared — the doves and vultures story in Chapter 7. He was very receptive to the story, probably because of previous rapport established using the *communication techniques* of reflective listening, I-messages, and open-ended questions.

Rapport and mutual respect also allowed instructors to suggest several books. Biographical stories added to Bob's *Super Hero's Closet*. A biography on Thomas Jefferson seemed particularly appropriate. The biography points out that Mr. Jefferson was in a social class that characteristically treated commoners with disdain, yet one of Jefferson's most admirable traits was the respect he extended to all people, rich or poor. Role models in Bob's Super Hero's Closet would also help *counteract backsliding* — a return to his cutting ways.

As a final piggybacked technique, a *behavior contract* was set up. Several adventuresome backpacking trips offered at Deer Crossing Camp require that campers pass an interview process. One characteristic the mountain guides look for is positive, supportive behavior. Bob wanted very much to go on one of these trips. In his first interview, the mountain guides set up a contract. If Bob displayed supportive behavior for the next two weeks at camp, they would consider him for an ascent team in a later session.

Within weeks of piggybacking motivational techniques, Bob's negative criticism stopped and he became a supportive member of our camp family. Almost overnight, he went from being a negative and critical individual who others avoided to a teen capable of being supportive and constructive in his comments. Campers now went out of their way to seek his company.

While one motivational technique might be effective, combining as many techniques as possible — piggybacking — is the best way to guarantee motivational impact. In Bob's case we used: perspective, reinforcing feedback, feedback to change behavior, magic keys, experience in place of words, communication skills, Super Hero's Closet to counteract backsliding, and discipline.

Quality motivation and piggybacked methods can also benefit kids who have a lot going for them. In the following example of combining motivational techniques, fill in the blanks with the technique being described (answers at end of story):

SPEECHLESS

Susan is a super-teen. She is energetic, happy, socially skilled, and bright. As a leadership candidate at Deer Crossing Camp, she was ready to tackle many challenges. One of those challenges was learning to speak in front of an audience. In phobia lists, speaking to a group ranks at the top. Susan had this fear, but piggybacked motivation techniques would help her overcome her speaking anxiety.

First, Susan felt an overwhelming sense of dread about speaking. She said, "I can't do it." The instructor shared a story with Susan, the T'NACI story (Chapter 7). What motivational technique is this? _____

Second, Susan took a book with blank pages and wrote down what she hoped to accomplish by speaking: "I want to deliver a three-minute talk in front of twenty people." She then took some binder paper and made an outline that included what she would talk about, when she would talk, who she would talk to, how she would get information for the talk, and where she would talk. What technique? _____

Third, the speech process was broken down into bite-sized chunks. For instance, the first session involved physical presentation. What physical characteristics give a speaker poise? Susan learned five simple traits displayed by confident speakers: stance, smile, eye contact, gestures, and voice modulation. She then worked on each aspect until she had it mastered. What motivational technique is being employed here?

_____

Fourth, as Susan practiced the various parts of the speech process, she was corrected with specific improvements: "Susan, maintain eye contact with individuals in the audience for five to seven seconds before shifting to someone else." When Susan showed improvement, she received specific praise: "Using those mime gestures focuses me on what you are saying." What technique? _____

Fifth, Susan was given the responsibility of explaining features of the program to new campers. What technique? _____

Susan overcame her fear and was speaking to groups of thirty by the end of camp. When Susan left, she took her new self-confidence with her. Back in high school, she credited her speaking experience with giving her the courage to direct a school play. Piggybacking motivational techniques is a powerful strategy for helping teens.

(Answers: 1. Attitude story, 2. Goal Steering, 3. Needs: Achievement (blanket training), 4. Self-Esteem: Feedback, 5. Self-Esteem: Power.)

A bicycle enhances your power. Bikes rely on combined parts to increase mechanical efficiency. *No More Nagging, Nitpicking, & Nudging (A Guide To Motivating, Inspiring, and Influencing Kids Aged 10-18)* enhances your persuasion power. This book relies on combined methods to increase your motivational efficiency. The complementary methods presented are designed to work together. To maximize your effectiveness, use all the techniques. Think of them as one tool, similar to a bicycle.

Happy pedaling.

APPENDICES

Biographical Books, Tapes And Videos For The Super Hero's Closet

Have your teenagers go through the following appendices and circle books, audio cassettes, and videos they are interested in. Order or pick up one of these resources this week.

APPENDIX 1: BOOKS

Biographical series written specifically for young people include:

The Childhood of Famous Americans Series. Aladdin Books, Macmillan Publishing Co., 866 Third Avenue, New York, NY 10022. Easy reading for children seven and up. Concentrates on the childhoods of famous people. Adults will also find these books informative and interesting. Available titles include:

Susan B. Anthony	*Robert E. Lee*
Crispus Attucks	*Abraham Lincoln*
Clara Barton	*Annie Oakley*
Daniel Boone	*Molly Pitcher*
Davy Crockett	*Paul Revere*

Thomas A. Edison	*Knute Rockne*
Albert Einstein	*Teddy Roosevelt*
Henry Ford	*Betsy Ross*
Benjamin Franklin	*Babe Ruth*
Lou Gehrig	*Jim Thorpe*
Helen Keller	*George Washington*
John F. Kennedy	*Martha Washington*
Martin Luther King, Jr.	*Wilbur & Orville Wright*

Solutions: Profiles in Science for Young People. Barron's Educational Series, 250 Wireless Blvd., Hauppauge, NY 11788. Suitable for ages 12 and up. These biographies tell about both the people and the discoveries that made them famous. Scientific information is presented in a simple format. Available titles include:

Marie Curie and the Discovery of Radium
Charles Darwin and the Theory of Natural Selection
Thomas Edison: The Great American Inventor
Albert Einstein and the Theory of Relativity

Dell Yearling Biographies. Bantam Doubleday Dell Publishing Group, Inc., 666 Fifth Ave., New York, NY 10103. Suitable for ages 10 and up. Available titles include:

Annie Sullivan, Helen Keller's Teacher
George Bush: The Story of the Forty-First President of the United States
Marching to Freedom: The Story of Martin Luther King, Jr.
Shirley Temple Black, Hollywood's Youngest Star
The Story of Alexander Graham Bell
The Story of Jackie Robinson
The Story of Sacajawea
The Story of Louisa May Alcott
The Story of Muhammad Ali

Women of Our Time. Puffin Books published by Viking Penguin, 40 West 23rd Street, New York, NY 10010. Suitable for seven and up. The qualities mentioned in the books should go into both boys' and girls' Super Hero's Closets. Available titles include:

Mary Bethune: Voice of Black Hope
Shirley Temple Black: Actress to Ambassador
Julie Brown: Racing Against the World
Carol Burnett: The Sound of Laughter
Rachel Carson: Pioneer of Ecology
Babe Didrikson: Athlete of the Century
Betty Friedan: A Voice for Women's Rights
Dorothea Lange: Life Through the Camera
Juliette Gordon Low: America's First Girl Scout
Margaret Mead: The World Was Her Family
Our Golda: The Story of Golda Meir
Grandma Moses: Painter of Rural America
Martina Navratilova: Tennis Power
Mother Teresa: Sister to the Poor
Dolly Parton: Country Goin' to Town
Eleanor Roosevelt: First Lady of the World
Diana Ross: Star Supreme
Beverly Sills: America's Own Opera Star
Margaret Thatcher: Britain's "Iron Lady"
Laura Ingalls Wilder: Growing Up in the Little House

Minstrel Books published by Pocket Books, a division of Simon and Schuster, 1230 Avenue of the Americas, New York, NY 10020. Suitable for 12 and up. Large type, illustrations, and photos make these books easy to digest. These autobiographies are on contemporary people such as Harvey Kurtzman, the founder of MAD Magazine. Even adults will find the books interesting. Available titles include:

My Life As An Astronaut: Alan Bean
My Life As A Cartoonist: Harvey Kurtzman
My Life With The Dinosaurs: Stephen and Sylvia Czerkas

Great Lives. Fawcett Columbine Book, published by Ballantine Books, produced by the Jeffrey Weiss Group, Inc., 96 Morton Street, New York, NY 10014. Suitable for 11 and up. Available titles include:

Christopher Columbus: The Intrepid Mariner
Amelia Earhart: Challenging the Skies
John Glenn: Space Pioneer
Mikhail Gorbachev: The Soviet Innovator
Jesse Jackson: A Voice for Change
John F. Kennedy: Courage in Crisis
Martin Luther King: Dreams for a Nation
Abraham Lincoln: The Freedom President
Sally Ride: Shooting for the Stars
Franklin D. Roosevelt: The People's President
Harriet Tubman: Call to Freedom

APPENDIX 2: TAPES

(As a source for additional cassettes, in addition to those listed below, refer to the comprehensive bibliography of audio cassettes found in *R.R. Bowker On Cassette*, 1989, R.R. Bowker, New York.)

Darwin and the Beagle, Alan Moorehead. Books on Tape Inc., P.O. 7900, Newport Beach, CA 92658. (714) 548-5525 or (800) 626-3333. Six cassettes. Darwin's voyage aboard the Beagle was a true Indiana Jones saga. He explored jungles and islands in search of exotic creatures and strange bones from the past. His enthusiasm for knowledge laid a new foundation for the science of biology.

Grinding It Out: The Making of McDonalds, Ray Kroc. Newstrack, 1055 W. Arizona, Denver, CO 80223. (303) 778-1692 or (800) 525-8389. A 52-year old milkshake machine salesman starts one of the biggest corporations in the world.

John Madden-Hey Wait A Minute (I Wrote a Book), John Madden. Newstrack, 1055 W. Arizona, Denver, CO 80223. (303) 778-1692 or (800) 525-8389. Two cassettes. John Madden's football coaching career. Anecdotal stories of his philosophy for developing the championship Raider's football team. Tells of the long years necessary to become a coach. Examples of player commitment and the inimitable Madden humor.

Lee Iacocca, Lee Iacocca. Nightingale-Conant Corp., 7300 N. Lehigh Ave., Chicago, IL 60648. (312) 647-0300 or (800) 323-5552. How Lee Iacocca became President of Chrysler Motors.

Lincoln, Gore Vidal. Random House, 201 E. 50th St. New York, NY 10022. (212) 751-2600 or (800) 638-6460. Why would Lincoln visit a hospital ward filled with enemy confederate soliders?

Rosalynn Carter: First Lady From Plains, Rosalynn Carter. Books on Tape Inc, P.O. 7900, Newport Beach, CA 92658. (714) 548-5525 or (800) 626-3333. What's it like to be first lady in the White House?

Running Free, Sebastian Coe. Listen Pleasure, 1 Columbia Dr., Niagara Falls, NY 14305. (716) 298-5150. Two cassettes. The story of Sebastian Coe who broke three world running records in 41 days. Explains the stresses of competition at the higher levels and the sacrifice to become a gold medal winner at the Olympics.

The Amateurs, David Halberstram. Dove Books on Tape, 12711 Ventura Blvd, Suite 250, Studio City, CA 91604. (818) 762-6662 or (800) 345-9945. Two cassettes. The effort of four young men intent on going to the Olympics as rowing entrants. Focuses on the perseverance needed in a little known sport. Mentions many names. Anecdotes are few and far between. Includes the realistic touch of covering some contestants who work very hard but don't make the final cut.

The Autobiography of Benjamin Franklin, read by Ed Begley. Caedom Records, 1995 Broadway, New York, NY 10023. (212) 580-3400. Two cassettes. The wisdom of this founding father has a fresh ring to young ears. Ben had a tough time getting his career started at 12 years of age, but the philosophy he developed still rings of common sense.

The Cosby Wit, His Life and Humor, Bill Adler. Dove Books on Tape, 12711 Ventura Blvd, Suite 250, Studio City, CA 91604. (818) 762-6662 or (800) 345-9945. Did you know that Bill Cosby dropped out of high school? Of even more significance, did you know that he recognized the importance of education and received not only his high school diploma but completed a college degree at the height of his career?

The Mick, Mickey Mantle. Newstrack, 1055 W. Arizona, Denver, CO 80223. (303) 778-1692 or (800) 525-8389. Two cassettes. The story of Mickey Mantle and his career in baseball. Shows what it takes to become the best and how you have to handle the setbacks in life in order to reach the top.

The Story of My Life, Helen Keller. 1987 Audio Book Contractor Inc., P.O. 40115, Washington, D.C. 20016. (202) 363-3429. The beauty of the world as seen through blind eyes.

Up From Slavery. Afro-Am Publishing Co. Inc., 819 S. Wabash Ave., Rm. 610, Chicago IL 60605. (312) 922-1147. Story of Booker T. Washington's boyhood, struggle for education, and influence as a man.

APPENDIX 3: VIDEOS

(As a resource for additional videos, in addition to those listed below, refer to: *The Video Source Book,* David J. Weiner (editor). 1990. Gale Research Inc.)

Abe Lincoln in Illinois. 1940. Fox Hills Video, 2730 Wilshire Blvd., Suite 500, Santa Monica, CA 90043. (213) 829-7441.

Alexander the Great. 1956. MGM/UA Home Video Inc., 10000 W. Washington Blvd., Culver City, CA 90232-2728. (213) 280-6000.

Ansel Adams: Photographer. Pacific Arts Video, 50 North La Cienega Blvd. Beverly Hills, CA 90211.

Autobiography of Miss Jane Pittman, The. 1974. Prism Entertainment, 1888 Century Park E., Suite 1000, Los Angeles, CA 90067. (213) 277-3270.

Einstein (NOVA). 1979. Vestron Video. P.O. Box 4000, Stamford, CT 06907.

Gandhi. 1982. RCA/Columbia Pictures Home Video, 2901 W. Alameda Ave., Burbank, CA 91505.

Great Americans: Martin Luther King Jr. 1982. Britannica Films, 310 S. Michigan Ave., Chicago, IL 60604. (312) 347-7958.

Great Americans: Thomas Jefferson. 1980. Britannica Films, 310 S. Michigan Ave., Chicago, IL 60604. (312) 347-7958.

Great Americans: George Washington. 1980. Britannica Films, 310 S. Michigan Ave., Chicago, IL 60604. (312) 347-7958.

Great Americans: Benjamin Franklin. 1980. Britannica Films, 310 S. Michigan Ave., Chicago, IL 60604. (312) 347-7958.

Great Americans: Andrew Jackson. 1982. Britannica Films, 310 S. Michigan Ave., Chicago, IL 60604. (312) 347-7958.

Great Americans: Abraham Lincoln. 1982. Britannica Films, 310 S. Michigan Ave., Chicago, IL 60604. (312) 347-7958.

MacArthur. 1977. MCA Home Video, 70 Universal City Plaza, Universal City, CA 91608. (818) 777-4300.

Masters of Comic Book Art, The. 1989. Rhino Home Video, 2225 Colorado Ave., Santa Monica, CA 90404.

Mother Teresa. Today Home Entertainment, 9200 Sunset Blvd., PH9, Los Angeles, CA 90069. (213) 278-6490 or (800) 877-8434.

Norman Rockwell's World ... An American Dream. Home Vision. 1-800-262-8600.

The Miracle Worker. 1962. MGM/UA Home Video Inc., 10000 W. Washington Blvd., Culver City, CA 90232-2728. (213) 280-6000.

Tom Edison, the Boy Who Lit Up the World. 1978. Children's Video Library, 60 Long Ridge Rd., P.O. 4995, Stamford, CT 06907. (203) 968-0100.

Young Winston. 1972. RCA/Columbia Pictures Home Video, 3500 W. Olive Ave., Burbank, CA 91505. (818) 953-7900.

Annie Oakley. 1985. Playhouse Video, 1211 Ave. of the Americas, New York, NY 10036. (212) 819-3238.

Alexander Graham Bell: The Voice Heard Round the World. 1984. AIMS Media Inc., 6901 Woodley Ave., Van Nuys, CA 91406-4878. (818) 785-4111 or (800) 367-2467.

Lou Gehrig Story, The. 1956. Discount Video Tapes Inc., 833 "A" N. Hollywood Way, P.O. 7122, Burbank, CA 91510. (818) 843-3366.

Will Rogers: The Cowboy Humorist. 1954. Two Star Films Inc., P.O. Box 495, Saint James, NY 11780. (516) 584-7283.

BIBLIOGRAPHY

Adams, James. *The Care and Feeding of Ideas: A Guide to Encouraging Creativity.* Reading, Massachusetts: Addison-Wesley Publishing Co., Inc., 1986.

Bandler, Richard and John Grinder. *Reframing: Neuro-Linguistic Programming and the Transformation of Meaning.* Moab, Utah: Real People Press, 1982.

_____. *The Structure of Magic: A Book About Language and Therapy.* Palo Alto, California: Science and Behavior Books, Inc., 1975.

Blanchard, Kenneth and Spencer Johnson. *The One Minute Manager.* New York: William Morrow and Company, Inc., 1982.

Brookes, Mona. *Drawing With Children: A Creative Teaching and Learning Method That Works for Adults, Too.* Los Angeles: Jeremy P. Tarcher, 1986.

Cialdini, Robert B. *Influence: The New Psychology of Modern Persuasion*. New York: Quill, 1984.

Clark, Aminah; Harris Clemes; and Reynold Bean. *How to Raise Teenager's Self-Esteem*. Los Angeles: Price Stern Sloan Inc., 1978.

Dilts, Robert. *Applications of Neurolinguistic Programming*. Cupertino, California: Meta Publications, 1983.

Dinkmeyer, Don and Gary McKay. *The Parent's Guide: STEP/Teen, Systematic Training for Effective Parenting of Teens*. Circle Pines, Minnesota: American Guidance Service, 1983.

Dodson, Fitzhugh. *How to Discipline With Love: From Crib to College*. New York: NAL Penguin Inc., 1977.

Elkind, David. *All Grown Up and No Place to Go: Teenagers in Crisis*. Reading, Massachusetts: Addison-Wesley Publishing Co., 1984.

Faber, Adele and Elaine Mazlish. *How to Talk So Kids Will Listen & Listen So Kids Will Talk*. New York: Avon Books, 1982.

Fisher, Roger and Scott Brown. *Getting Together: Building a Relationship That Gets to Yes*. Boston: Houghton Mifflin Co., 1988.

Gallatin, Judith. *Adolescence and Individuality: A Conceptual Approach to Adolescent Psychology*. New York: Harper and Row, 1975.

Gardner, Howard. *Frames of Mind: The Theory of Multiple Intelligences.* New York: Basic Books Inc., 1985.

Garfield, Charles. *Peak Performers: The Heroes of American Business.* New York: Avon Books, 1986.

Ginsburg, Herbert and Sylvia Opper. *Piaget's Theory of Intellectual Development: An Introduction.* New Jersey: Prentice-Hall Inc., 1969.

Labinowicz, Ed. *The Piaget Primer: Thinking, Learning, Teaching.* Menlo Park, California: Addison-Wesley Publishing Co., 1980.

Laborde, Genie Z. *Influencing With Integrity: Management Skills for Communication and Negotiation.* Palo Alto, California: Syntony Publications, 1983.

McClelland, David. *Human Motivation.* New York: Cambridge University Press, 1987.

Melton, David. *Survival Kit for Parents of Teenagers.* New York: Saint Martin's Press, 1979.

Peters, Thomas and Robert Waterman. *In Search of Excellence: Lessons from America's Best-Run Companies.* New York: Warner Books, Inc., 1982.

Von Oech, Roger. *A Kick in the Seat of the Pants.* New York: Harper and Row, 1986.

York, Phyllis; David York; and Ted Wachtel. *Toughlove.* New York: Bantam, 1982.

INDEX

ABOUT THE
AUTHOR

At fourteen, my parents encouraged me to get a job. I decided to offer swim lessons in the family pool. The swim school was my first practical class in motivation: I learned how to help youngsters and adults overcome fears of deep water, how to guarantee swimming success in the shortest possible time, and methods of inspiring competitive swimmers. By eighteen, I had learned and earned enough to purchase property and move the swim school out of my parents' backyard.

Two of my mentors, Olympic coaches Art Lambert and Pete Cutino, passed along practical motivation strategies when I swam and played water polo for them. Later, I became a coach myself. As the University and Provincial Coach for water polo in British Columbia, I was voted most valuable coach at the Canadian National Championships. The feedback techniques described in Chapter 3 were responsible for raising our senior team to Western Canadian Champions and our junior team to national champions.

Later, I was elected vice president of Canadian Coaching Certification for water polo.

While working toward a Master's degree in biology, I earned a living instructing laboratory classes, tutoring students, and lecturing. This was an opportunity to practice motivation in an academic setting.

After graduating, I became involved in projects that utilized motivation in a management environment. As a marine biologist, I was involved with underwater research projects. Later, as head chemist for a Silicon Valley corporation, I coordinated installation of high tech engineering projects.

While I enjoyed research and working in industry, I eventually shifted my focus to a dream shared by my family.

For years, my parents had talked about developing a summer camp dedicated to nurturing potential in children. In 1976, my parents, brother, sister, and our two labrador retrievers started laying the groundwork for *Deer Crossing Camp Inc.* Six years later we opened. Our wilderness lodge and location are similar to a Sierra Swiss Family Robinson experience. Whether a child is from San Francisco, Paris, New York, Sydney, or Tokyo, living at Deer Crossing is an adventure: 100 square miles of wilderness at the back door, an azure blue lake at the front door, and the nearest road two miles away. Our staff come from all over the world to teach windsurfing, kayaking, art, canoeing, guitar, Tae Kwon Do, improvisational comedy, sailing, backpacking, and more. For many teens, a summer at camp coincides with a time in their lives when they are actively assembling a personality. Deer Crossing's motivational philosophy is designed to promote the best in teens. The techniques described in this book are standard operating practice at Deer Crossing Camp.

In addition to being a camp director, I write articles and lead workshops on motivating children. My award-winning column on teens appears in the *Bay Area Parent News Magazine*, and reprints appear regularly in parenting publications across the nation. As a columnist, I meet parents, teens, educators, and coaches to ask questions about what works and what doesn't. I incorporate this information into articles and workshops. Two workshops, **Motivating Kids to Motivate Themselves** and a workshop for teens entitled **You Can Lead**, cover techniques described in this book.

If you are interested in seminars, workshops, or finding out more about Deer Crossing Camp, call **(408) 996-9448** or write to our office:

Deer Crossing Camp, Inc.
P.O. Box 486
Cupertino, California 95015

No More Nagging, Nit-picking, & Nudging

A guide to motivating, inspiring, and influencing kids aged 10-18

Jim Wiltens is to the parents of teens what Dr. Spock was for so many years to the parents of babies.
Bay Area Parent News Magazine

____ Copies pbk. $9.95

Goal Express!
Turn Your Dreams Into Reality

Learn the 5 skills used by successful goal-setters

... this book will benefit anyone who wants to do more than dream about life's adventures.
John Goddard. First explorer to kayak the entire Nile river

____ Copies pbk. $9.95

Please send ____ books x $9.95/book = ____

Postage and handling ($1.75 for first book plus $1.00 for each additional copy). = ____

California residents add sales tax of 72¢/book. = ____

Make check or money order payable to *Deer Crossing Press*. No cash or CODs please.   Total = ____

Mail books to:

Name: _____

Address: _____

City: _____State: ____ Zip: _____

Phone: (_____) _____

Send this form with your payment to:

Deer Crossing Press
690 Emerald Hill Rd.
Redwood City, CA 94061